PRETEEN DEVOTIONAL FOR BOYS

PRETEEN DEVOTIONAL FOR BOYS

52 WEEKS OF SCRIPTURE AND GUIDANCE

SHANE HANSEN

Zeitgeist • New York

ISBN: 9780593690130
Ebook ISBN: 9780593689943

Illustrations © by VectorPixelStar/Shutterstock.com
Book design by Aimee Fleck
Author photograph courtesy of the Hansen family
Edited by Kim Suarez

Printed in the United States of America
1st Printing

FOR MY BOYS

Christian, Isaiah, Elijah, and Jonathan

INTRODUCTION

You might be wondering why a guy in your age group needs his own devotional. Well, for starters, you're at a time in life when changes are happening—big-time. You're not exactly a kid anymore; not exactly an adult. You might be wondering about all kinds of things. Like fitting in. Or standing out. Or how you're supposed to act or think or feel, not to mention where God fits into it all.

So this book is designed especially for you. The weekly Bible verses and messages will help you gain a better overall understanding of God's character and heart, as well as your own call to a life worthy of the name "Christian."

God's Word, the Bible, is the central focus of each devotional, and the messages and prayers will give insight to help you use what you learn in your everyday life. Each week, we'll focus on a topic that most of us encounter on the journey toward manhood. You'll be encouraged to expand your thinking and open your heart to God's message of love and salvation through Jesus Christ.

Ten years from now, you'll be a man. This time in your life—yes, *right now*—is special. You're ready to start deciding what kind of person you want to be. You are a member of the next generation of Godly men, and you will one day be a leader of God's people. Take this to heart. Read the Bible verses and lessons each week. Spend time thinking through the "Go Deeper" questions. This is all for you. You are important. You are loved.

As we prepare to start this journey together, think about this passage from 2 Timothy:

> *"But as for you, continue in what you have learned and have become convinced of, because you know those from whom you learned it, and how from infancy you have known the Holy Scriptures, which are able to make you wise for salvation through faith in Christ Jesus. All Scripture is God-breathed and is useful for teaching, rebuking, correcting and training in righteousness, so that the man of God may be thoroughly equipped for every good work."* (2 Timothy 3:14–17)

All Scripture is God-breathed. That means that everything in the Bible is there because God wanted it to be there for you to read and know. Take time to understand how awesome that is, and let God's words soak in so that you can be equipped for all of the amazing, good works God has in store for you.

God's blessings to you, today and always!

GOD'S GAME PLAN FOR MY LIFE

"For I know the plans I have for you," declares the Lord, "plans to prosper you and not to harm you, plans to give you hope and a future."

JEREMIAH 29:11

If you've ever played on a sports team or watched a game on television, you've probably seen coaches using a game plan to help lead their team to victory. Dedicated coaches put in hours preparing game plans—studying game film, reviewing player performance, and doing whatever it takes to ensure the team is ready for game day.

Our Bible verse this week demonstrates that, like a coach preparing a game plan for his team, God has plans for your future as well. The phrase *"plans to prosper you and not to harm you"* is an assurance that God desires good things for you and those words also serve as a promise from God that if you stick to his ways and his will while executing his "game plan" for your life, you will have success (prosper), and he will not lead you into trouble (harm).

But that's only half of the story about God's game plan for your life! The second half of God's promise to you in this verse is that he has *"plans to give you hope and a future."* Like a good coach, God has studied *you* deeply, and he has plans that will put you in the best possible position to be successful in not only a game but your entire life.

Now, those are some great reasons to be excited to play your game of life, both now and in the future!

1. The God who created you and the entire universe around you cares so much about *you* that he has lovingly developed plans for your life. What gives you hope about your future?

2. What other Bible verses or stories help you to better understand God's plans for your future? How do these contribute to your faith and trust in God?

3. Just like the ups and downs during a game, there will be times in life when it will feel like things aren't going your way—even when you are trying to live in line with God's will. Don't give up during those times! Remember, on Good Friday, the disciples didn't understand why Jesus had to die. But with our longer view of history we now know that on the third day he rose again. Trust God's promises for the plans that he has for your life, even if you can't always see how things could turn out for the best at certain points during the journey. Through Jesus Christ we are assured that if it's not good, it's not the end!

PRAYER

Dear heavenly Father, please help me to continue to learn about the promises you make to me in the Bible, and to always trust in the plans that you have for my life. I know that through Jesus, I have already "won." Help me to always keep that hope as the focus of my life. In Jesus's name, amen!

THAT'S THE WAY GOD MADE ME

"For you created my inmost being; you knit me together in my mother's womb. I praise you because I am fearfully and wonderfully made; your works are wonderful, I know that full well."

PSALM 139:13–14

Did you ever wonder why you look a certain way? Maybe you wonder why you are so short, or tall, or big, or small . . . or why you have curly hair, freckles, or green eyes. Well, there are some hereditary factors involved in how you look (like if both of your parents have curly hair then you will probably have curly hair too). But the simple answer to why you look the way you do is that God designed you that way.

Sometimes, other people might tease you about things that you can't control (such as your height, your skin complexion, or the way your voice sounds), but we know that we are beloved children of God. (Check out Romans 8:16.) And if he made us this way, if he created our inmost being and knit us together before we were born, then we don't have to worry about what others might say about us, because we know that we can be proud of ourselves, just the way we are. If someone teases you about the way you look, just tell them, "That's the way God made me."

Be proud of who you are and how you look. The God who created all things loves YOU so much that he made you the unique person that you are. His works (including you) are wonderful, and we know that full well.

1. What are three things that are unique about how you look?

2. How do those three unique things about you point to God's wonderful design?

3. How does it feel knowing that the same God who designed and created all of the unique/beautiful things in this world took the loving care to also create the unique/beautiful (handsome) things about you?

PRAYER

Dear God, thank you for loving me so much that you designed me to be one of a kind, not only in the way I look but also in the interests and abilities that you have blessed me with. Please help me to always have confidence in the way that I look, knowing you made me this way—and to be kind to all other people, since I know that they are lovingly created by you as well. In Jesus's name, amen.

He Knows

"All the days ordained for me were written in your book before one of them came to be."

PSALM 139:16

Have you ever tried to predict the future? Depending on the situation, you might be able to make some pretty good guesses. For example, you might say that the weather will be warmer in the summer, or that you will get hungry in the evening. But those are easy, because seasons and even eating schedules follow predictable patterns based on the year or time of day. Those aren't really *predictions* about the future, as something like a prediction that you will score the winning point in the championship game your senior year of high school. The winning point prediction is more descriptive, more distant, and not tied to any usual daily or seasonal cycle.

Our Bible verse this week tells us that God knows about each one of the days in your life before you even live them. It's not even a prediction in this case, because the verse tells us that God already *knows* what your future holds. You aren't a robot, so you get to choose the paths that you go down and the decisions that you make each day, but God loves you so much that he is working all things for your good and nudging you to pursue the paths that lead to your most blessed life on earth, as well as (through Jesus) eternal life in heaven.

God has a book with the story of your life written in it, and it is one of his all-time favorite stories to read! He has the book, but he still gives you the ability to be the author and to choose the adventures you will add to the pages each day. God loves you so much that through Jesus, he weaves *your* story together with *his* story. That's a lot to take in, right? But instead of worrying about all of these details and about your future, instead simply rest in the knowledge that God cares deeply about you and trust him when he tells you that through his Son, Jesus Christ, your story is one that will move forward with the words, "and he lived happily ever after."

1. What is your favorite book? Why?

2. What is going on in your life story right now?

3. How have you noticed God helping you write your life story?

4. How does it make you feel, knowing that God has a book with your life story written in it, and that through Jesus, your story will never end but go on happily ever after in heaven?

PRAYER

Heavenly Father, thank you for caring for me so much that you have the story of my life written in your book. I trust you to help me write my life story and look forward to seeing where you lead me on this journey. I give thanks and praise to you in Jesus's name, amen.

BE BRAVE WITH GOD

"Be strong and courageous. Do not be afraid or terrified because of them, for the Lord your God goes with you; he will never leave you nor forsake you."

DEUTERONOMY 31:6

The definition of BRAVE is "ready to face and endure danger or pain; showing courage." When this week's verse tells you to be strong and courageous, it is essentially telling you to be brave.

Strong + Courageous = Brave.

The next sentence encourages you not to be afraid or terrified because of them. Who is *them*? Well, that can be any person or thing that is potentially terrifying to you. Maybe it's a math test, a music performance that you have coming up, or a game against the biggest and best team in your league. Whatever the current "them" is in your life, God's Word is telling you not to be afraid or terrified.

Words can be uplifting, but in the face of a challenge they sometimes fall flat. Actions, however, speak louder than words—and in this verse, God demonstrates real action that you can count on. "God goes with you; he will never leave you nor forsake you." Think about the biggest, strongest bodyguard walking with you wherever you go. And think about the promise that your bodyguard is eternally loyal, meaning that he will NEVER leave you or fail you.

But, you might say, I don't *see* God walking with me. How can I be brave when bad or scary things still come my way? That's a deeper topic we'll get into later, but for now, just remember that Jesus tells us, "And surely I am with you always, to the very end of the age" (Matthew 28:20). We know that God is 100 percent trustworthy—so when he tells us that he will be with us always, we can trust that even if we don't see him, he is there. He comes through the presence of the Holy Spirit, or through angels who help us (Psalm 91:11), and even through the unseen presence of Jesus himself. We don't always know (or see) all the ways that God is with us, but the bottom line is that when we trust in him, we can be strong and courageous because we are never alone.

1. What does it mean to be brave?

2. Who are some people you know, or people from history, who have shown bravery? How?

3. What has helped you to be brave when you're feeling afraid?

4. How can you lean more into God's promises and presence to help you be brave?

PRAYER

Dear God, thank you for your promises in the Bible that reassure me that I can be brave no matter what I am facing in my life. Help me to remind myself of your love and presence whenever I start to feel afraid. Thank you for the hope and assurance that I have in Jesus— today, tomorrow, and forever. Amen.

GOD IS MY SOURCE OF HOPE AND STRENGTH

"He gives strength to the weary and increases the power of the weak. Even youths grow tired and weary, and young men stumble and fall; but those who hope in the Lord will renew their strength. They will soar on wings like eagles; they will run and not grow weary, they will walk and not be faint."

ISAIAH 40:29–31

What an uplifting passage this week! First, let's look at the challenges presented in these verses: weary, weak, tired, stumble, and fall. The burdens and stressors of life can be a lot for anyone to withstand, even "youths" and "young men," two groups of people who are known to have lots of energy and strength. We *all* face challenges and sometimes feel tired and weak. But those challenges are just the first half of the equation. Wait for it . . .

Those challenges are met with the following responses: strength, power, hope, soar, and run. Just think how encouraging each day would be if you lived with strength and power, and if you had the undefeated energy to soar and run. And this passage says that you *do* have those abilities!

We all face challenges and get worn down in life, but the way to beat those trying times is to place our hope in God. When we do that, he gives us strength, power, hope, and the energy to soar and run.

So, how do you hope in the Lord? You trust that God will always see you through every challenge that comes your way, and you believe Jesus when he tells us to "Come to me, all you who are weary and burdened, and I will give you rest" (Matthew 11:28).

God is our source of hope and strength. Believe it, trust in him, and live with that confidence every day of your life!

1. When have you been tired and weary?

2. How have you been able to persevere through challenges, or how would you use the Bible passages from this week to help you press on through challenges that come your way?

3. How does it make you feel to think about being able to place your hope in God, and in turn, knowing that he will help you to soar and run?

PRAYER

Heavenly Father, Son, and Holy Spirit, I thank you for assuring me that I can put my hope in you, and that you will help me get through any challenges that I may face in life. Help me to be confident that I will have the strength and power to overcome, and that through your presence in my life, I will be able to soar and run! In Jesus's name, amen.

HOW SHOULD I SPEND MY TIME?

"Teach us to number our days, that we may gain a heart of wisdom."

PSALM 90:12

When you're growing up, it seems like you are always surrounded by people who are teaching you something. Just think, you learn from your parents/guardians, grandparents, teachers, coaches, pastors . . . But for all of that learning, if I asked you to describe the things that God wants us to spend our time on, would you know how to answer?

I'm guessing many people would say that God wants us to love and serve others and to spread the good news of Jesus. Sure, that sounds like a great answer. But what does that mean in your everyday life?

Let's get back to the first word in this week's verse: *teach*. How does God teach us things? For starters, he has given us his Word—the Bible. When we spend time reading the Bible and reflecting on its lessons, we are being directly taught by God.

Let's play that out further. If we read the Bible to learn how God wants us to spend our time, we'll find that there are many answers to that question—as many as there are people on earth! That's because God prepares and calls *each* of us to live and serve in our own unique ways. There isn't a one-list-fits-all answer. That's where the "gain a heart of wisdom" part comes in. When you study and think about God's Word, God will work wisdom into your heart and help you understand how he is uniquely calling you to spend the time he has blessed you with.

1. What are some lessons that you have been taught that have helped you gain wisdom?

2. What lessons have you learned from God? How?

3. In what ways do you feel God calling you to number your days (spend your time)?

4. Spending time reading and reflecting on the Bible is important. Can you commit to spending some time with your Bible each day? What time of day will you do this?

PRAYER

God, thank you for giving me your Word and a spirit to understand it. Help me learn to use both together to learn how you want me to spend my time. Please help me to gain a heart of wisdom, and to bring honor and glory to you through the way that I live my life. Amen.

ABOUT LOVE

"Love is patient, love is kind. It does not envy, it does not boast, it is
not proud. It does not dishonor others, it is not self-seeking, it is not
easily angered, it keeps no record of wrongs. Love does not delight
in evil but rejoices with the truth. It always protects, always trusts,
always hopes, always perseveres. Love never fails . . . And now these
three remain: faith, hope and love. But the greatest of these is love."

1 CORINTHIANS 13:4–8, 13

What would you say if someone told you that they have a 100 percent
surefire answer to everything? Sounds too good to be true, right? But that
is exactly what we receive in this week's Bible passage.

Love is the answer.

It has been said that if you try to summarize the entire Bible into one
word, that word would be "LOVE." The Bible is the story of God's love for his
creation (which absolutely includes YOU), and how he gave his only Son,
Jesus Christ, to be our Savior (1 John 4:9–10). And what's more, the Bible
tells us that God actually *is* love (1 John 4:7–8).

Love is the answer.

So, what is love? In this week's Bible passage, we learn that love is
patient and kind, and that it rejoices with the truth. We also find out that
love does not envy or boast and that it is not proud, self-seeking, or easily
angered. Love doesn't keep a record of wrongs or delight in evil.

This passage uses the word "always" several times when discussing
what love is. It says that love "always protects, always trusts, always hopes,
always perseveres." When we see an absolute word like "always," we know
that thing being described is certain 100 percent of the time. If it only was
true 99 out of 100 times, then it wouldn't qualify as being "always." So we

know that love ALWAYS protects, trusts, hopes, and perseveres. Those are solid qualities that we can build our understanding of love on. Interestingly, another absolute word is used to describe what love *never* does . . . that's right, love "never fails." Again, we have 100 percent certainty with love!

When everything else is stripped away, three things remain: faith, hope, and love. "But the greatest of these is love."

Love is the answer to why God created you. Love is the answer to why you can trust in Jesus as your Savior. Love is the answer when you are wondering how you should treat other people.

Love is the answer!

1. Why do you think this week's study talks about love being the answer to everything?

2. How does the description of love in this week's Bible passage help you to better understand what love is and what it is not?

3. How does it make you feel to understand how deep God's love is for you?

4. What are some ways that you can demonstrate love to the people in your life?

PRAYER

God of love, thank you for loving me so much that you gave your Son, Jesus Christ, to be my Savior. Thank you for teaching me that love is the greatest and that it never fails, and please help me to live my life with that understanding as I continue to grow into a loving young man. Amen.

BEING, AND FINDING, A GOOD FRIEND

"Do to others as you would have them do to you."

LUKE 6:31

"Rejoice with those who rejoice; mourn with those who mourn."

ROMANS 12:15

Do you remember the first time you ever made a friend? Maybe it was a kid in your daycare or preschool class, someone from Sunday school or your sports team, or possibly it was a kid you met through your parents or guardians. Whatever the case, it's always exciting (and a little scary sometimes) to meet people and make new friends.

How do you know when you've made a new friend? Typically, you find out that you have something in common with another person—like a shared interest in a certain sport, video game, or book—and then you start talking about that. Soon, you start to share experiences like playing in the park, having lunch together, or talking about things you both like to do. Eventually, you build trust and feel a connection with each other. You look forward to hanging out and doing things together.

Let's step back for a minute. How do you choose who you want to be friends with? Maybe they share an interest like a sport or video game, or see the world the way you do. Maybe they're funny or nice or silly. While you may look for all sorts of things in a friend, there's one thing that's really important: kindness. You want to be around people who treat you kindly. In our first verse this week, Jesus says that we should "do to others as you would have them do to you." Sounds pretty simple, right? But it is really important with friendships. You want to be treated kindly, and it is equally important that you treat others that way too. If you see someone playing by themselves on the playground, you could ask if they want to join a game that you and your friends are playing. That's how you would want to be treated if you were alone, right? And if you didn't like it when someone teased you about your haircut, remember that for when someone else has a similar situation, and be sure to be kind to that person instead of teasing them. That's what good friends do.

Our second verse about friendship talks about being there for your friends in good times *and* in bad times. Rejoice with them when they are happy, and be there for them when they are sad. Your good friends will do the same for you.

Friendship is a blessing, and as a friend, you can make a positive impact on another person's life. So go out and be a great friend today!

1. What qualities do you look for in friends?

2. What's an example of how you treat others the way you want to be treated?

3. How have you rejoiced and mourned with your friends?

PRAYER

Dear Lord, thank you for the friends that you have brought into my life. Please help me to keep making friends who will be positive influences, and help me be the same for them. Show me how I can demonstrate your love through the way that I treat others. I give thanks and praise to you always in Jesus's name, amen.

FITTING IN

"Do not love the world or anything in the world. If anyone loves the world, the love for the Father is not in him. For everything in the world—the cravings of sinful man, the lust of his eyes and the boasting of what he has and does—comes not from the Father but from the world. The world and its desires pass away, but the man who does the will of God lives forever."

1 JOHN 2:15-17

Do you like to fit in, or would you rather stand out? Some people like to be different and thrive in the spotlight. But most people are more comfortable blending in with the crowd. Our verse today, however, challenges us *not* to go along with the crowd.

You see, the crowd in this verse means the "world" and the things of the world, like "the cravings of sinful man, the lust of his eyes and the boasting of what he has and does." But what does that mean?

In a nutshell, it means putting things like wealth, power, and material comforts first in our lives—even ahead of love and kindness and doing what's right. It means desiring something—like a fancy vehicle, a large home, or an impressive title—in an unhealthy way. And it means bragging about it all. It's not a good look, and this verse is telling us that those types of attitudes come from the "world," not God.

It also says that the "world and its desires pass away, but the man who does the will of God lives forever." So, following our sinful nature will lead to destruction—to "passing away" out of God's presence. But living a life in keeping with God's ways will lead us closer to him and to heaven.

Now, we are all human. We make mistakes and fall short. We're not perfect and we can't "earn" our way into heaven. But God loves us so much that he sent Jesus to show us the way back to him. Bottom line, trust in Jesus Christ as your Savior and you will live forever in heaven!

So look for courage to go against the trends of this world and live with God as the center of your life instead. You will stand out from the crowd, and you can use that spotlight to shine bright for Jesus!

1. What are some examples of things this verse would describe as "the world"?

2. How do the people who do God's will stand out from the crowd?

3. What are some ways that you can demonstrate the fruits of the Spirit (love, joy, peace, patience, kindness, goodness, faithfulness, gentleness, and self-control) in your life?

PRAYER

Heavenly Father, thank you for teaching me about the difference between the will of the world and your will. Forgive me for the times when I have gone along with the world, and give me the strength to live a life that bears the fruit of the Spirit. Help me to let your light shine in this world so that I can encourage others to do your will and to know Jesus. Amen.

PREPARING FOR BATTLE

"Finally, be strong in the Lord and in his mighty power. Put on the full armor of God, so that you can take your stand against the devil's schemes . . . Stand firm then, with the belt of truth buckled around your waist, with the breastplate of righteousness in place, and with your feet fitted with the readiness that comes from the gospel of peace. In addition to all this, take up the shield of faith, with which you can extinguish all the flaming arrows of the evil one. Take the helmet of salvation and the sword of the Spirit, which is the word of God. And pray in the Spirit on all occasions with all kinds of prayers and requests."

EPHESIANS 6:10-11, 14-18

It's neat to learn about knights and battles, isn't it? We have a natural element of competition ingrained in us. We compete to get into certain schools, to win a game, and to earn the love of that special someone. These days, competition doesn't often lead to death. But in war, and for those knights of old who wore the fancy armor and carried swords and shields, the stakes were very high—win and live, lose and die.

It's a story as old as time—the battle of good versus evil—and whether you realize it or not, you are currently engaged in the most important battle of all time. Now, you might not be wearing the heavy metal armor of a knight, but our verses this week paint the picture of the *spiritual* armor you are equipped with.

The devil wants to trick you into believing his lies and deceptions so that you will deny God and give in to your sinful nature. Don't fall for the enemy's traps—and watch out for those "flaming arrows" he's shooting at you!

Let's take a closer look at the armor of God. Imagine that you walk into God's military camp and that some of the other knights and angels are there, outfitting you and your friends with God's armor. They equip you with a belt of truth that will hold the rest of your outfit together.

Next comes the breastplate of righteousness, which is the right way to live. This will protect your heart. It is essential that you physically keep your heart safe and spiritually keep your heart pure.

Another group of godly servants comes to make sure that your feet are "fitted with the readiness that comes from the gospel of peace," which means that when you walk with the Lord, he will light your paths (Psalm 119:105) in the direction of peace.

The shield of faith comes next and is used to "extinguish all the flaming arrows of the evil one." A steadfast faith serves us well, and we can use it to block the devil's attacks.

Finally, a helmet of salvation is dropped onto your head, and a sword of the Spirit is placed in your hand. The helmet protects your mind and thoughts. The sword serves as a reminder that you have the Holy Spirit with you, fighting for you.

You are now ready for battle.

But wait! Before you face the battlefield, a last important instruction is whispered into your ear. "Don't forget, young man, that to stand firm through this battle and come out victorious, you must pray in the Spirit on all occasions with all kinds of prayers and requests. That is our 'secret weapon,' not that we will fight this battle on our own, but that we have the faith and humility to call upon God for his almighty strength and protection."

Stand firm, young knight. The battle is upon you, but you are fully equipped to come out victorious. Godspeed!

1. What part of the armor of God stood out the most to you? Why?

2. Have you felt yourself equipped with this armor at certain times in your life? If so, how?

3. How is spiritual warfare the same or different from physical warfare?

4. How can you recognize the attacks of the enemy, the devil, when they come your way?

PRAYER

Lord, I know I can't fight the spiritual attacks of the enemy on my own. But I also see that you have equipped me to stand firm in this fight as I use the armor you have equipped me with. Guide my steps as I move forward into the next days and years of my life so that I may stand victorious with you through your Son, my Savior, Jesus Christ. Amen.

WHEN a LOVED ONE DIES

> "If you declare with your mouth, 'Jesus is Lord,' and believe in
> your heart that God raised him from the dead, you will be saved.
> For it is with your heart that you believe and are justified, and it
> is with your mouth that you profess your faith and are saved . . .
> Everyone who calls on the name of the Lord will be saved."

ROMANS 10:9–10, 13

> "Jesus answered him, 'I tell you the truth, today
> you will be with me in paradise.' "

LUKE 23:43

It's always difficult when a loved one dies. Whether they're an older person with health issues or a younger person, such as a parent or a friend, it's hard to say goodbye and can be very difficult to understand. Eventually, we learn that life goes on for those of us still here in the earthly chapter of our lives.

However—and, my friend, this is a very big HOWEVER—we as Christians know that our life on earth is just one chapter of our much bigger *eternal* life that continues beyond this world. Through Jesus, we know that once God calls us home to be with him, we will be reunited with our loved ones who are already in heaven.

The first of this week's Bible verses explains that when we declare our faith in Jesus, God credits to us Jesus's perfect life and his victory over death and sin. Because of Jesus paying the price for us, we get to go home to heaven after our lives on earth are complete.

Yes, this is a lot to digest, but I know you are ready to start to understand the beauty in God's story for our lives on earth and in eternity in heaven.

In the second verse this week, a criminal who was hanging on a cross next to Jesus asked Jesus to "remember me when you come into your kingdom." Jesus says the man will be welcomed to heaven that very day, and he speaks those same words to you and me and to all who believe in him. We can trust that when it is our time to be called home by God, we will be able to join our loved ones in paradise.

1. Read this week's verses from Romans 10 out loud. Now think about what you just said. YOU ARE SAVED THROUGH JESUS CHRIST! How does that make you feel?

2. Who are some well-known Christians from history who you expect are in heaven right now?

3. Heaven is described in other passages of the Bible as a place where there are no more tears, where we will be in constant fellowship with God, where the streets are made of gold . . . In our second verse this week, Jesus used one word to describe heaven: "Paradise." What are some aspects of heaven that you are excited about?

PRAYER

Jesus, thank you for standing in as a perfect sacrifice in the place of all who believe in you, so that when it's time to leave this world, we can come home to heaven and be with you there. Please help me to continue to grow in my understanding of, and faith in, the eternal journey of life. Amen.

WHAT SHOULD I THINK ABOUT AND DO?

"Set your minds on things above, not on earthly things."

COLOSSIANS 3:2

"Everything is permissible"—but not everything is beneficial. "Everything is permissible"—but not everything is constructive. Nobody should seek his own good, but the good of others."

1 CORINTHIANS 10:23-24

Imagine your life is like a blank chalkboard. You walk up to it and grab a piece of chalk. But now comes the tricky part—what do you want to write or draw on the board? Do you want to devote the board to your favorite sports team or favorite food, or to something that is taking up your thoughts at the moment, like an upcoming test? Or do you want to divide the board into eight equal sections and write about eight different topics—a well-rounded approach? There are lots of options on how to fill up the chalkboard, but ultimately it's your decision.

Our lives are kind of like that blank chalkboard. God created us and gave us *free will*, which means we are not robots. We have the power to make our own decisions and control our own actions. But God didn't just leave us alone without any directions. He gave us his written Word, the Bible, to read and study, and he also sent us the Holy Spirit to live with us and serve as our guide.

This week, we are focusing on two Bible verses that talk about how God wants us to live our lives—and fill in our blank chalkboards. In the first verse, we are encouraged to think about godly things, not earthly things. This can mean that we focus on things such as bringing honor and glory to God, serving others, and spreading the good news of Jesus Christ—heavenly things—instead of earthly things, like the latest celebrity gossip or political news.

Our second verse tells us that just because everything is allowed, that doesn't mean that it is necessarily right for us. If you aren't sure if it's a good idea to eat or do something, pray about it. I could drink 12 sodas in one night, but is that good for me? I could skip church to play video games, but is that good for me? It's not complicated, but it is important that we put some thought into how we fill in our blank chalkboards—our lives. How will you design your chalkboard masterpiece?

1. What are some "things above" that you can take some time to think about each day?

2. How can you tell the difference between things that are appealing to you and things that are good for you? What's the difference between those two types of things (appealing versus good for you)?

3. How can you get a better understanding of how God wants you to spend your time and energy each day?

PRAYER

Heavenly Father, sometimes I struggle to do the right thing, but I know that I am forgiven when I ask for your mercy, and that your Son Jesus Christ has washed my mistakes away. Help me to continue to grow in my understanding of how you want me to think and what you want me to do with my life. Thank you for your blessings and for the fresh opportunities that each day brings. Amen.

WHO I AM

"To one there is given through the Spirit the message of wisdom, to another the message of knowledge by means of the same Spirit, to another faith by the same Spirit, to another gifts of healing by that one Spirit, to another miraculous powers, to another prophecy, to another distinguishing between spirits, to another speaking in different kinds of tongues, and to still another interpretation of tongues. All these are the work of one and the same Spirit, and he distributes them to each one, just as he determines."

1 CORINTHIANS 12:8–11

We are all blessed with both physical and spiritual gifts. You probably have started to understand some of your physical gifts—like if you can run really fast, paint detailed pictures, or are talented at playing a musical instrument. Physical gifts can be easier to identify than spiritual gifts. But spiritual gifts are just as important (maybe more so) as physical gifts, and as we read in our Bible passage this week, they are given to us by the Holy Spirit.

Here is a summary of the spiritual gifts that we heard about in our 1 Corinthians passage:

- Wisdom
- Knowledge
- Faith
- Healing
- Powers
- Prophecy
- Discernment
- Ability to Speak Languages (Tongues)
- Interpretation of Language (Tongues)

Have you recognized any of these spiritual gifts in yourself? Identifying and understanding your spiritual gifts can be a process that takes years to unlock. As you continue to grow and develop into a young man, your "superpowers" (spiritual gifts) will start to become more recognizable, both by you and those whom you spend time with. A pastor, counselor, friend, or parent/guardian are all people who might be able to help you over the next few years as you begin to understand your spiritual gifts. Isn't it neat to think about how you have been blessed with really special gifts that you haven't discovered yet? Every day of your life will be a journey of further growth and understanding in your relationship with God, and growing into your spiritual gifts is one way that this relationship deepens.

1. What are some physical gifts that you have been blessed with?

2. What are some spiritual gifts that you have been blessed with?

3. What are some things that you can do to use your physical and spiritual gifts at the same time?

4. Who are two people you can talk with to help you better understand your spiritual gifts?

PRAYER

Dear Lord, it's awesome to keep learning more and more about myself, and how you have uniquely created me both physically and spiritually. Help me as I continue to unpack these gifts, and show me how I can use them to serve you throughout my life. In Jesus's name I pray, amen.

WHAT IS GOD'S WILL?

"Now listen, you who say, 'Today or tomorrow we will go to this or that city, spend a year there, carry on business and make money.' Why, you do not even know what will happen tomorrow. What is your life? You are a mist that appears for a little while and then vanishes. Instead, you ought to say, 'If it is the Lord's will, we will live and do this or that.' "

JAMES 4:13–15

Do you know what the Lord's Prayer is? In chapter 6 of the book of Matthew, Jesus teaches his disciples how to pray, and this prayer is known as the "Lord's Prayer." In it, part of what Jesus, speaking to God the Father, says is, "your kingdom come, your will be done." To this day, this is one of the most recited prayers among Christians.

Your kingdom come, your will be done. What does that mean? It means seeking God's kingdom and his will over our own earthly interests. Since we are followers of Jesus, just like those early disciples were, we should strive to live this way as well.

Our verse this week from James reminds us that our lives on this earth are temporary, and instead of boastfully declaring how we are going to spend our time, we should instead first bend a knee to God and acknowledge that *if* it is his will ("will" means "desire" in the way we are talking about it here), we would like to do this or that. The other side of that stance means that if we find out (through prayer or some other way) that something we want to do is *not* God's will, then we should change course and pursue God's will over our own desires.

How do you do that? Action one: Pray. Action two: Talk with other brothers and sisters in Christ (people who are Christians) and ask them to help you understand whether something is God's will or not. The more you practice doing those two things as you seek to follow God's will in your life, the more you "will be able to test and approve what God's will is—his good, pleasing and perfect will" (Romans 12:2).

1. Open your Bible to Matthew 6, and read the Lord's Prayer. What does this prayer make you think about?

2. Why is it important that we seek to follow God's will instead of our own desires?

3. Have you ever felt God nudging you to make a certain decision or do a certain thing? Do you think that was an example of God communicating his will to you?

PRAYER

God, I love you and I want to know more about your will. I want to follow your desires for my life and honor you in the way that I think and act. Please help me to learn more about your will as I read the Bible, and as I feel the Holy Spirit leading me in my life. In Jesus's name, amen.

WHO'S NUMBER ONE?

"So the last will be first, and the first will be last."

MATTHEW 20:16

"Do nothing out of selfish ambition or vain conceit. Rather, in humility value others above yourselves, not looking to your own interests but each of you to the interests of the others."

PHILIPPIANS 2:3-4

Have you ever noticed how, on different social media platforms, a lot of what is posted is a sort of competition to one-up other people's posts? Surf around online sometime and you'll find that there isn't a whole lot of humility or putting others first in most people's posts.

In our Scripture verses this week, we see that this self-promotion approach to life is not what God wants for us. In the first verse, Jesus is telling us that when we put ourselves first, we will actually be last in God's eyes. Likewise, in the second verse, Paul encourages us to be humble servants to others out of devotion to Christ. Going back to the example of social media, how much different would some people's posts look if they followed Paul's advice and considered others better than themselves? I bet we'd see lots of posts congratulating others—singing their praises and celebrating their accomplishments.

". . . not looking to your own interests but each of you to the interests of the others." How often do you see your friends and classmates (and if you are being honest, yourself too) letting someone else go in front of them in line or getting the biggest dessert, or being willing to settle for a lesser role on a team or in a play so that another person gets the opportunity to shine?

Humility isn't a character trait that our culture teaches, celebrates, or values. But remember, *God* values things much differently than humans do. God wants us to be loving, and love is not self-seeking.

It is good to work hard and to be proud of your accomplishments, but you should also strive to make sure that you give God the glory and that you seek to uplift others too. God knows the great things that you do, and his praise is worth more than any human applause ever could be.

1. What is one example of someone in the Bible demonstrating humility?

2. Can you think of a time when you acted with humility in your own life?

3. What are some ways that you can intentionally act with humility in the week ahead?

PRAYER

Heavenly Father, Son, and Holy Spirit, please help me to look for ways that I can humbly serve you in my life. Sometimes, that may mean that I intentionally put others ahead of myself, and sometimes, it might mean that I quietly do something behind the scenes to brighten some-one else's day. God, help me to seek your praise rather than pursuing any earthly recognition or awards. You are all that I need! Amen.

ABOUT CRUSHES

"Flee the evil desires of youth and pursue righteousness, faith, love and peace, along with those who call on the Lord out of a pure heart."

2 TIMOTHY 2:22

Maybe you've experienced the sensation already—that lighthearted feeling that comes when a girl you like walks into the room or says hi to you. God sees value in romantic relationships. After all, in Genesis, we read about God creating Adam, the first man, and then going on to create the first woman, Eve, to be with him.

Maybe for now, you'd rather play football or video games than bother with all that romantic stuff. But over the next few years, you may start to feel differently. For instance, some of the things girls do that you thought were annoying might start to seem cute. Where you once saw an ordinary classmate, you might start seeing beauty. And when you look into that special someone's eyes, you may feel your heart start to pound. The truth is that God created boys in a way that, as they become young men, they begin to have romantic desires. It's all part of God's plan!

Our verse this week talks about the "evil desires of youth." What are these evil desires? Well, they could include the fighting that boys and girls do at early ages. Then sometimes during the teen years, the physical body develops faster than the emotional senses. During this time period, boys and girls might have some physical desires to act as husbands and wives do, but they are not yet emotionally mature enough to handle those situations. Our verse this week simply tells us to "flee" those desires. How do you do that? Treat your special someone with honor and respect, the way you would if Jesus himself were there in the room with you.

The rest of our verse talks about what you *should* do: pursue righteousness, faith, love, and peace "along with those who call on the Lord out of a pure heart." That's important. As you begin to enter into romantic relationships, remember that *any* relationship, whether you're "just friends" or romantically inclined, will have the best possible chance to flourish if you and the other person share the same values. This creates a strong foundation to build the relationship on.

And maybe you will find that as you become a young man, you will start choosing to spend more of your time with your special someone. Who knows? Maybe she'll even like football and video games just like you do! ☺

1. What are some examples of how you have shared things such as righteousness, faith, love, and peace with other people in your life?

2. Do you have any friends (boys or girls) who have values similar to yours? If so, how does that form a strong foundation in your relationship?

3. Do you have a crush or like anyone in particular? What are some qualities about this person that you appreciate?

PRAYER

Dear God, thank you for making so many beautiful things in this world, including the interesting and unique ways that you have made boys and girls. As I continue to grow and develop both physically and emotionally, help me to find the right ways to pursue righteousness, faith, love, and peace with others who call on your name from a pure heart. I ask these things in Jesus's name, amen.

ALL DAY LONG

"Rejoice always; pray continually; give thanks in all circumstances, for this is God's will for you in Christ Jesus."

1 THESSALONIANS 5:16-18

There are 24 hours in a day, and typically, you divide those hours into several main activities. Breakfast, school, practice, homework, supper, sleep, and so on. When you complete one task, you move on to the next. There are very few things that you would do *continuously* throughout the day. Can you think of anything that you do continuously all day long, other than breathing?

Our Bible passage today identifies several things that we should do *all* the time.

1. **Rejoice always**—Jesus tells us not to let our hearts be troubled (John 14:1). When you strive to live joyfully (with an untroubled heart), your whole outlook changes, creating exciting opportunities and experiences in your life. Rejoice always, and trust in God and Jesus.

2. **Pray continually**—What does it look like to *pray continually*? It means that you are always mindful of God's presence. You might make a conscious effort to bring prayer into your activities throughout the day, or train yourself to approach life as one long prayer that goes on and on. Either way, the message is clear—we are called to pray *continually*.

3. **Give thanks in all circumstances**—If you are rejoiceful always and praying continually, it's going to be awfully hard *not* to be giving thanks in all circumstances. If your approach to life is aligned with the first two sections of this Bible verse, then your heart will be grateful, no matter what—even grateful for things you don't like. That's because with faith, you know that God is working for your good *all* of the time (Romans 8:28)—and that's definitely a great reason to give thanks in all circumstances.

Rejoice always, pray continuously, and give thanks in all circumstances; it's a three-part activity that you can try to do all day long. If you approach life this way, you will experience living with the joy of the Lord in your heart always. And that's a great way to live!

1. What's one way that you can intentionally be rejoiceful always?

2. How can you get in the habit of praying continually? (Maybe start before eating each meal, and then try to expand it to something that you do before or after other activities throughout your day.)

3. Challenge yourself to give thanks to God as often as you can remember to do so each day this week. What do you think you will learn, or feel, when you start doing this regularly?

PRAYER

Father God, help me to follow your game plan for how I can approach every aspect of life throughout my days. Thank you for giving me examples of things I can do to be full of joy, stay connected with you through prayer, and give thanks to you always. Amen.

unseen peace

**"Now faith is being sure of what we hope for
and certain of what we do not see."**

HEBREWS 11:1

They say seeing is believing—and sometimes that's true. We *see* that grass grows, so we *believe* we'll eventually need to mow it. But sometimes, we believe in things we can't see. We can't see gravity, but when we throw a ball up in the air, we know it will come back down. Thus, we believe that gravity is real. What about love? You can't see love, but when someone is consistently kind to you—when they tell you they love you, and when you trust them fully—you can believe in love, even if you can't see it or measure it.

Our verse this week tells us that faith is one of those things that we can be certain about, even when we don't see it. In fact, we are told that faith is being sure of what we hope for. This reassurance gives us a sense of unseen peace that we can build our lives on.

Are you familiar with the story of "Doubting Thomas"? Thomas was one of Jesus's disciples, but he wasn't there the first time Jesus visited his friends after he had risen from the dead. Thomas couldn't believe Jesus could really be alive again—he'd have to see him in the flesh to believe it (John 20:25). A week later, Jesus visited again, and this time, Thomas was there. When he saw Jesus with his own eyes and was able to touch him, Thomas said, "My Lord and my God!" *Now* he had enough evidence to believe. What Jesus says next is important to our study this week. "Because you have seen me, you have believed; blessed are those who have not seen and yet have believed" (John 20:29).

Our verse this week and the story of Doubting Thomas both reassure us that we can be confident in God even if we don't see him. Learn this week's verse. Use it whenever you have a Doubting Thomas kind of moment. God is real, and he loves you very much! Knowing that brings the peace of God, which is too wonderful to understand (Philippians 4:7). We can't see it, but we can feel it.

1. Read 1 Corinthians 13:13. What makes you believe in unseen things such as faith, hope, and love?

2. People who are physically blind have to rely on things other than a sense of sight to understand the world around them. As a child of God, how can you develop your faith in the things of the Spirit that you can't see, touch, or measure?

3. What is one thing that you confidently hope for (have faith in) as a follower of Jesus Christ?

PRAYER

Dear Lord, every day there are things that I experience that I can't physically see—like gravity, or a breeze blowing through my hair, or maybe sometimes a feeling of your presence. Thank you for assuring me that I can be confident in you even when I don't see you, and please help me to continue to grow my faith in Jesus, my Lord and Savior. Amen.

Learning Important Lessons

"For the message of the cross is foolishness to those who are perishing, but to us who are being saved it is the power of God. For it is written: 'I will destroy the wisdom of the wise; the intelligence of the intelligent I will frustrate.' Where is the wise person? Where is the teacher of the law? Where is the philosopher of this age? Has not God made foolish the wisdom of the world? . . . For the foolishness of God is wiser than human wisdom, and the weakness of God is stronger than human strength."

1 CORINTHIANS 1:18-20, 25

As a student, you are learning a wide range of important lessons. Math, history, science, reading, and writing . . . Those lessons will undoubtedly help you to accomplish many things in your life. But none of them will prepare you to earn or achieve eternal salvation for your soul. Jesus Christ alone can provide that for you.

The most important lesson you'll ever learn is that you need a savior. We all sin—we all take wrong turns and make mistakes. But Jesus died for our sins so that even though we aren't perfect, our eternal life in heaven is 100 percent secure.

Not everyone agrees with our view about salvation. In fact, our verse this week explains that to people who are lost, "the message of the cross" seems like foolishness. That's a big difference of opinion! There are people in this world who think they know it all and who scoff at God and his lessons, but our reading says that God will teach *them* a lesson by destroying their supposed wisdom.

Think about where you'd rather stand: With the limited wisdom of humans, or with the unlimited wisdom of God—who is so deep that we cannot even begin to fathom his majesty. I know which side I'll be standing on. "Choose for yourselves this day whom you will serve . . . but as for me and my household, we will serve the Lord" (Joshua 24:15).

1. There are people in this world who are pretty smug in their confidence in their own wisdom. They view it as their own greatness and don't believe God has played a part in it. Here are a couple of additional verses that address God's view of people with this type of attitude. "Although they claimed to be wise, they became fools . . ." (Romans 1:22) ". . . always learning but never able to acknowledge the truth" (2 Timothy 3:7). How can you tell the difference between earthly knowledge and godly knowledge?

2. What is "the message of the cross"?

3. What are your favorite subjects to learn about? How do you think you will use your knowledge of those subjects in the future?

PRAYER

God, you are so much bigger, deeper, grander, and more mysterious than I can even begin to imagine. Yet I know that you love and care about me. Help me to learn as much as I can about all of the interesting topics in this world, but to never put anything ahead of my learning about, and love for, you. You are awesome, God, and I praise you for all of your blessings. Amen.

DEALING WITH BULLIES

> "Do not repay anyone evil for evil. Be careful to do what is right
> in the eyes of everyone. If it is possible, as far as it depends on
> you, live at peace with everyone. Do not take revenge, my dear
> friends, but leave room for God's wrath, for it is written: 'It is mine
> to avenge; I will repay,' says the Lord. On the contrary: 'If your
> enemy is hungry, feed him; if he is thirsty, give him something
> to drink. In doing this, you will heap burning coals on his head.'
> Do not be overcome by evil, but overcome evil with good."
>
> ROMANS 12:17–21

Actions speak louder than words. We've all met people who say one thing but then act in an opposite manner. After that happens a few times, you start to lose respect for the person. Sure, it's easy to say all the right things, but if their actions don't back up their words, then why should you listen to them, right?

It would be pretty easy to dismiss our Bible verses this week as nothing more than idealistic talk. Should we really give our enemy food and drink just to "heap burning coals on his head" (make him madder)? Or overcome evil with good? Does that stuff actually work? Our instincts tell us if someone is being mean to us, that we should repay them by being mean back to them.

But if we look closer at this week's reading, we see that the words really do match up with the example that Jesus set for us during his life. In Matthew chapter 5, Jesus teaches that we should love our enemies and pray for those who are mean to us. That certainly seems contrary to what our natural response would be, but yet those are the words of our teacher. And Jesus backed up those words with actions. Think about this: Jesus did not resist arrest, willingly died on the cross for crimes he did not commit, and as the Roman soldiers were abusing and insulting him, do you know what he said in response? "Father, forgive them, for they do not know what they are doing" (Luke 23:34). He prayed for them!

I hope you never have to deal with a bully—and it might be challenging for you to be perfect in your response to one. But you can try to follow the words from this week's Bible reading, and you can try to follow the ultimate example of Jesus himself. And remember, you don't have to face bullies alone. If someone is picking on you, in addition to praying for them, you should tell a trusted adult, like a teacher, pastor, or parent/guardian. Together, you and that trusted adult will be able to come up with a plan to address a bully.

1. What kind of bullying situations have you or someone you know had to deal with? How have you/they handled those situations?

2. What would it feel like to love your enemy and pray for those who persecute you?

3. Why do you think God wants you to respond to bullies this way?

PRAYER

Heavenly Father, there are times when other people mistreat me and make me sad or angry. I know you teach us to love our enemies, but that can be hard. Help me to live at peace with everyone, but if I'm ever in conflict with another person, help me to handle it in a way that brings honor to you. In Jesus's name I pray, amen.

THE HOLY SPIRIT LIVES IN ME

"But very truly I tell you, it is for your good that I am going away. Unless I go away, the Advocate will not come to you; but if I go, I will send him to you . . . I have much more to say to you, more than you can now bear. But when he, the Spirit of truth, comes, he will guide you into all the truth."

JOHN 16:7, 12–13

"Do you not know that your bodies are temples of the Holy Spirit, who is in you, whom you have received from God?"

1 CORINTHIANS 6:19

It was very difficult for the disciples to understand. How could it be "good" that Jesus was going away? Jesus had been their teacher and friend for the past three years, and they believed that he was the Messiah—the Son of God who would restore God's kingdom on earth. How could Jesus's leaving possibly be for their good?

Now, more than 2,000 years later, we can see what Jesus meant when he said that it would be for the good of the disciples and all of his followers in the years to come (including you and me) if the Advocate, the Holy Spirit, would come to them. You see, Jesus is both God and man. During his earthly ministry, he was human, so he could only be in one physical place at a time. But the Holy Spirit is able to be with *all* of God's people *all* the time, which is good. It means we all can have constant fellowship with God through the Holy Spirit.

Our second verse this week talks about how the Holy Spirit lives inside of us and guides us in all truth. That means the Spirit reminds us of Jesus's teachings, nudges us to do or say what is right, and inspires us to live the kind of lives God wants for us. Some people say that we all have a conscience, which tells us when we do something wrong. Christians believe that this "conscience" is actually the Holy Spirit reminding us of right and wrong and guiding us to live godly lives. So, we believe that the Holy Spirit is God's presence with us always.

I told you these were difficult truths to understand. First, that it could be for our good that Jesus had to leave the earth, and second, to grasp the concept of the Holy Spirit actually living in us. Difficult to understand, yes, but important and true—*also* yes. I pray that you seek the Holy Spirit to guide you and comfort you all the days of your life.

1. Why does Jesus describe the Holy Spirit as the "Advocate"?

2. Have you felt the Holy Spirit teach or lead you in your life? If so, what was the situation, and how did you know it was the Holy Spirit?

3. If your body is a "temple of the Holy Spirit," how do you think you should take care of it?

PRAYER

Holy Spirit, thank you for coming to me and for being my constant godly companion and Advocate through this life. I need you to help me make decisions that will bring honor and glory to you, God. Please help me to continue to understand your power and role in my life. Amen.

PEOPLE TO ADMIRE

"Do not consider his appearance or his height, for I have rejected him. The Lord does not look at the things people look at. People look at the outward appearance, but the Lord looks at the heart."

1 SAMUEL 16:7

You've probably heard the saying, "Don't judge a book by its cover." It's good advice. After all, there is no way of knowing how good or bad a book is just by the cover alone. The cover could be magnificent with beautiful illustrations and fancy lettering, but the story inside is rather boring. Or, the cover could be uninspiring, dull and drab, but the story inside might be the most fascinating thing you've ever read.

This lesson is shown in our Bible verse this week, which describes the scene when Samuel anointed David to be the next king of Israel. David had seven older brothers, many of whom looked quite impressive physically—especially compared side-by-side with their kid brother David. But as Samuel looked over all the brothers, trying to figure out which should be king, God said not to worry about what they looked like. "Man looks at the outward appearance, but the Lord looks at the heart."

How do you choose which people you admire? Is it based on the way they look? Or their accomplishments? Maybe you're a fan of a famous celebrity or a top athlete. It's not that there's anything wrong with paying attention to people who look good or who achieve impressive things. But remember that outward appearances and amazing accomplishments aren't the most important things to God because he "looks at the heart."

If you find yourself looking at someone's heart, pay close attention to what they say and do. Look for the fruits of the Spirit: love, joy, peace, patience, kindness, goodness, faithfulness, gentleness, and self-control (Galatians 5:22–23). When someone has the Holy Spirit living in their heart, you can see the fruit of the Spirit in the things that they say and do. If the heart is what matters to God, then it would be a good idea if we do the same when looking for people to admire.

1. Who are some people (famous or not) that you admire? Why?

2. Is it easier to look at the outward appearance or the heart of another person? Why?

3. Nutrients in fruits are good for the health of your heart. What are some things that you can do to get more daily servings of "fruit" (of the Spirit) in your life?

PRAYER

Dear God, thank you for teaching me that my heart is more important to you than my outward looks or accomplishments. Please help me to live in ways that reflect the fruit of the Spirit and that bring honor and glory to you. I ask this in Jesus's name, amen.

QUICK TO LISTEN AND SLOW TO SPEAK

"My dear brothers and sisters, take note of this: Everyone should be quick to listen, slow to speak and slow to become angry."

JAMES 1:19

Do you ever think about the human body and wonder why God designed us the way that he did? For example, why do most people have five fingers on each hand instead of four or six—and what's with fingernails? Or why do we have two eyes on the front of our head and none on the back? All mysteries to us, but we must trust that God had a good reason for everything.

Diving deeper into God's reasonings, I'm always fascinated by the possible answer to why God designed us with two ears and one mouth—it's been said that he created us this way so that we know to listen more than we talk.

This week's verse instructs us to be ready listeners and careful speakers. Here are two additional examples of Scripture supporting the notion that silence can be golden.

"The prudent keep their knowledge to themselves, but a fool's heart blurts out folly" (Proverbs 12:23).

"Even fools are thought wise if they keep silent, and discerning if they hold their tongues" (Proverbs 17:28).

Have you ever noticed that the letters in LISTEN are the same as the letters in SILENT? I don't know if there's any deep meaning to this, but it's interesting, right?

Now let's take a look at the final part of this week's verse: "slow to become angry." This makes sense. We would expect that Christian people would be able to control their tempers. But that's not always so easy to do, and we should continue to work hard to keep our anger in check.

According to Proverbs 14:29, "Whoever is patient has great understanding, but one who is quick-tempered displays folly." Great understanding is certainly a trait that will serve you well in your life. Understanding, patience, self-control—these are good, godly qualities. On the other hand, "a quick-tempered man displays folly" (folly means foolishness). A bit of advice: Most people don't want to be around someone who is quick-tempered and acts foolish. That's a combustible and dangerous combination, and not the way we are taught to live as people who serve Christ.

So act like a gentleman and control your emotions and actions by striving to be quick to listen, slow to speak, and slow to get angry.

1. What does it mean to be "quick to listen"?

2. What does it mean to be "slow to speak"?

3. What is one example from the Bible of a situation where someone was "slow to become angry"?

PRAYER

God of peace, thank you for giving me the lessons contained in your Word, the Bible. Help me continue to strive to live my life as a follower, and representative, of you. Please give me the patience, peace, and self-control to be quick to listen, slow to speak, and slow to become angry. I ask this in Jesus's name, amen.

LIFE TO THE FULL

"The thief comes only to steal and kill and destroy; I have come that they may have life, and have it to the full."

JOHN 10:10

Sometimes, people have the wrong impression of God. They see him as a cold, distant, hard-nosed ruler who gives his people a list of rules to follow and doesn't want them to have any fun or enjoyment in life. We know that's not true, and as Christians, we need to show people how vibrant, loving, and joyful God really is.

In our verse this week, Jesus makes it clear where he stands on the subject. "I have come that they may have life, and have it to the full." Jesus wants us to have full lives! Everyone can take pleasure in the many joys and beauties of this life, like the smell of freshly cut grass, the sound of a child's laughter, the sight of a beautiful sunset, the taste of a ripe strawberry, a hug from a loved one . . . All of these wonderful gifts are from God. "Every good and perfect gift is from above, coming down from the Father of the heavenly lights" (James 1:17).

But there's even more to this "life-to-the-full" living that God offers to us. So far, we have only mentioned earthly pleasures, and that's just scratching the surface of God's blessings. In addition to all of those good things, God also offers something far better—Jesus actually calls it *paradise* (Luke 23:43). Yes, I am talking about heaven—and what our lives will be like when we get there. If, for example, you think the colors in this world are beautiful, just imagine how much more vivid and striking the colors will be in heaven. This world only offers a glimpse of the true "life to the full" that we'll find in heaven with Jesus. (Check out 1 Corinthians 13:12.)

Now let's rewind and talk about the first part of this week's verse: "The thief comes only to steal and kill and destroy." Jesus was warning his followers not to be led astray by the devil's schemes or by some of the corrupt religious leaders of that time. We can still be led astray these days, can't we? We might think that it's more important to wear the right clothes, impress the right people, or hang out with the right crowd than it is to stick close to Jesus. We may sometimes feel like it's more important to get the approval of the popular kids than it is to seek God's approval. But if we want to have life—the fullest life—we need to choose Jesus, every time.

1. Describe what you think "life to the full" means.

2. Jesus describes heaven as paradise. What would paradise on earth look like to you? Now stretch your imagination, and describe what kinds of things you might experience in heavenly paradise.

3. What are some things that you can do to "live life to the full" this week?

PRAYER

Heavenly Father, you are awesome and I praise you for all of the amazing blessings that you give to me. Jesus, I want to thank you for coming to earth so that I may have life to the full. Please help me to stick with you in every choice I make, always. Amen.

THINGS MAY CHANGE, BUT GOD ALWAYS REMAINS THE SAME

"Jesus Christ is the same yesterday and today and forever."

HEBREWS 13:8

Change happens in one way or another every single day. Sometimes changes are so small that you don't even notice them, like your hair growing just a little bit longer each day. But what if you didn't get a haircut for a *whole year*? If you looked at pictures of your hair at the beginning and end of that year, I'm sure you would quickly see a big difference! Little changes each day can add up over time.

There are also big changes that happen in life. The day someone is born or dies brings big changes for those people and their loved ones. Or the day when a good friend moves away, when you start at a new school, or when your family gets a pet. These are just some of the many examples of big changes that can happen in life.

Some changes are welcomed; others bring heartbreak. But no matter what kinds of changes you face, remember that you have a firm foundation to stand on—one that never shifts or fails—and that's Jesus. Everybody encounters changes—good ones and hard ones—and everybody needs a solid base to build their life and identity on.

Change happens. It's part of life. But when it does, remember our verse this week, and know that your foundation, Jesus, is absolutely 100 percent secure.

1. James 1:17 tells us that "Every good and perfect gift is from above, coming down from the Father of the heavenly lights, *who does not change like shifting shadows.*" After reading this verse, along with Hebrews 13:8 and our Bible study this week, why do you think there are so many references in the Bible to let us know that God is consistent? Why is that important for us to know about God's nature?

2. How does it impact your faith in Jesus to know that he is the same yesterday and today and forever?

PRAYER

Dear Lord, thank you for being a firm foundation that I can build my life upon. When so much changes around me day-to-day and year-to-year, it is comforting to know your steady presence, promises, and love are always there for me no matter where I go in life. I can be confident today, tomorrow, and forever. Amen.

IT'S ALL GOOD WITH GOD

"And we know that in all things God works for the good of those who love him, who have been called according to his purpose."

ROMANS 8:28

Yes, it's all good with God. But that doesn't mean that *only* things that we view as "good" will happen in life.

What is your absolute favorite food to eat? Doughnuts, ice cream, pizza, steak, mac and cheese, something else? Imagine that you walk into a room and find an endless supply of that food, just the way you like it, sitting on a table. There's an empty plate and a chair waiting for you to sit down. How much of your favorite food do you think you would eat?

Now, imagine you have eaten about half as much as you'd planned when one of your parents or guardians walks into the room and tells you that you've had enough. Even though you are disappointed because you wanted to eat more of that delicious food, you know that this person loves you, so there must be a good reason why they are telling you to stop eating. (For example, maybe they know that if you eat too much, you'll get sick!)

This same dynamic helps us understand this week's Bible verse. "In all things, God works for the good of those who love him." That means that in everything that happens, if you love and follow God, he is working for your good. If your parent or guardian says YES, you can go to your friend's house, that's great, right? But if your parent or guardian says NO, you can't eat any more of your favorite food (because they know you'll get sick), that's great, too, isn't it? Because they love us, they want what's best for us.

The Bible tells us that God's thoughts and ways are different from ours—God's are higher (Isaiah 55:8–9). So if God's thoughts and ways are higher than ours, and he tells us that he is always working for our good, then we must try to trust that somehow, it is for the best when something doesn't go the way we wanted it to. That happened when Jesus died on the cross. His disciples could not understand it at the time, but three days later, when he walked out of that grave, they got it!

And God is working for your good in all things too, even if you can't always see it.

1. What are examples of things that you have seen or experienced that help you understand that God is working for your good?

2. What does it mean to love God and to be "called according to his purpose"?

3. How can you remind yourself that God is always working for your good, even when bad things happen in life? How does it make you feel to remember that?

PRAYER

Heavenly Father, Son, and Holy Spirit, thank you for always working for my good. Please help me to keep your promise in mind, even when I'm having a bad day. Your thoughts and ways are higher than mine, and when you tell me that in all things, you are working for my good, I can rest in that knowledge and trust in your love. Amen.

HOW SHOULD I PRAY?

"When you pray, say: 'Father, hallowed be your name, your kingdom come. Give us each day our daily bread. Forgive us our sins, for we also forgive everyone who sins against us. And lead us not into temptation.'"

LUKE 11:2-4

Have you ever played a game where the way to move ahead is by repeating a certain phrase or password? Typically, the scenario involves a "right" way to complete a set of actions or to say a sequence of words, which will then unlock the "next-level status," or simply the next step or a new level.

Prayer is sort of like that, but it is a much deeper process. At its purest level, prayer is simple and powerful. It is the opportunity for us to speak directly to God.

This week's verse is what Jesus said when one of his disciples asked him how to pray. This prayer has become known as the Lord's Prayer. Let's break it down:

"Father, hallowed be your name": This means that we should call on God the Father and show respect, love, and admiration for him and his name.

"Your kingdom come": God's kingdom is heaven, so if we call on his kingdom to come, we are calling for heaven to come to us.

"Give us each day our daily bread": "Daily bread" does include the food that we eat, but it is more than that. It also includes all of the things that we need in order to survive each day, like clothing, shelter, hope, and love. The key is to approach life one day at a time, and to pray for the "daily bread" each day—and not get caught up in praying for next week's bread before it's time. One day at a time, God will be faithful.

"Forgive us our sins, for we also forgive everyone who sins against us": When we make mistakes and are sincerely sorry, we can ask for God's forgiveness and know we'll receive it thanks to Jesus. Notice that Jesus also says that we should forgive those who sin against us. If we expect God's forgiveness for our mistakes, we must also be willing to forgive others.

"And lead us not into temptation": With this phrase, we are asking God to help us stay clear of temptations that could lead us to sin. We trust that when we follow God, he will lead us to good things and away from negative influences. (Read James 4:7–8.)

The Lord's Prayer serves as a wonderful outline for how we can pray. Remember that it is right and good to pray about all sorts of things and on every occasion (1 Thessalonians 5:17). It's fine to pray for a doctor's appointment to go well or for a loved one to get a job they are applying for. Prayer is the answer for any situation when we want to talk with God about our lives, or thank him for a blessing, or ask for his help. Prayer is an instant way to connect with God. If you don't know how to pray or what to pray about, try using the Lord's Prayer as a starting point, and God will open up the "next-level status" when you are ready to journey deeper into your prayer life with him. The key is to pray, pray, pray!

1. One approach to prayer that is widely taught is to P.R.A.Y. (Praise, Repent, Ask, Yield). Give it a try! Start a prayer by *praising* God for his love and goodness in your life. Next, *repent* your sins by saying that you are sorry for the mistakes you've made and ask for God's help to do better moving forward. Then, *ask* for anything that is on your mind (physical healing, blessing on a relationship, etc.). And finally, *yield*, which means earnestly desiring God's will to prevail.

2. Practice saying a prayer out loud that follows the P.R.A.Y. approach. How did it feel to pray that way?

PRAYER

Heavenly Father, thank you for loving me so much that you gave your son, Jesus Christ, to open the door for me to be able to communicate directly with you through prayer. Help me to continue to grow in my understanding of prayer, and to learn how to become more comfortable with praying to you. Thank you for caring about me so much that you listen to my prayers. Amen.

UNDERSTANDING WHO GOD IS

"Exalted to the right hand of God, he [Jesus] has received from the Father the promised Holy Spirit and has poured out what you now see and hear."

ACTS 2:33

You might have heard the word "Trinity" before, but it isn't a word that is mentioned in the Bible. Trinity is a word that was developed by people to try to describe God based on what we have learned about him in the Bible. Trinity means one God in three "persons"—Father, Son, and Holy Spirit. The word "Triune" is also used to describe the fellowship of the Trinity. Let's see what the Bible has to say about this fellowship.

Father and Son: "I and the Father are one" (Jesus speaking in John 10:30).

Father and Spirit: "Now the earth was formless and empty, darkness was over the surface of the deep, and the Spirit of God was hovering over the waters" (Genesis 1:2).

Son and Spirit: "It is for your good that I am going away. Unless I go away, the Advocate will not come to you; but if I go, I will send him to you" . . . "But when he, the Spirit of truth, comes, he will guide you into all truth" . . . "He will glorify me because it is from me that he will receive what he will make known to you. All that belongs to the Father is mine. That is why I said the Spirit will receive from me what he will make known to you" (Jesus speaking in John 16:7, 13, 14–15).

God in the plural sense: "Then God said, 'Let us make mankind in our image, in our likeness, so that they may rule over the fish in the sea and the birds in the sky, over the livestock and all the wild animals, and over all the creatures that move along the ground'" (Genesis 1:26). Notice the underlined words in this Bible passage. They are words that demonstrate God's presence as more than one component.

The concept of the Trinity is complex and difficult to understand—so don't feel bad if you're a little confused. It might help if you think about your own life. Are there at least three roles that you have? How about son, brother, cousin, friend, teammate? That isn't a perfect similarity to the three persons of God (nothing in this world would be), but it does show how someone could be one person with more than one function.

The most important thing is to keep trying to make sense of it as you read your Bible and build a better understanding of God. And remember, if Jesus tells us in his own words that we are to baptize "in the name of the Father and of the Son and of the Holy Spirit," then we can believe in the concept of a Triune God. Even if we can't fully understand, we can trust and believe based on faith.

"May the grace of the Lord Jesus Christ, and the love of God, and the fellowship of the Holy Spirit be with you all" (2 Corinthians 13:14).

1. In Exodus 3:14, Moses asked God what he should say to the Israelites when they asked who sent him. God answered, "I AM WHO I AM. This is what you are to say to the Israelites: 'I AM has sent me to you.'" How do you picture God when you think about him telling Moses that he is "I AM"? Do you picture God the Father, Son, or Holy Spirit—or picture him in some other way?

2. Our Triune God is difficult to understand. Believe in him based on faith, and remember what God tells us in Isaiah 55:9: "As the heavens are higher than the earth, so are my ways higher than your ways and my thoughts than your thoughts." Even when we don't understand, we can still believe.

PRAYER

Great I AM, while I don't fully understand your nature or presence, I believe that you are God, and that you have revealed yourself to humans as God the Father, Son, and Holy Spirit. Help me to continue to think about you as I grow closer to you throughout my life. Most importantly, help me to trust you and follow you, and to know that you love me and will always take care of me. In Jesus's name, amen.

THE ENEMY OF YOUR SOUL

"Be alert and of sober mind. Your enemy the devil prowls around like a roaring lion looking for someone to devour. Resist him, standing firm in the faith, because you know that the family of believers throughout the world is undergoing the same kind of sufferings."

1 PETER 5:8-9

Our enemy is real, and he is dangerous. He's also crafty and good at deception and lies. In fact, Jesus called him the "father of lies" (John 8:44). That's right, I'm talking about the devil. The world tries to make him into a fun, cartoonish character, but the Bible tells us that couldn't be farther from the truth. He is as nasty and hideous a being as there ever was or will be.

What does it mean that the devil is prowling around looking for someone to devour? It means that, ultimately, he hopes to get people to indulge in their sinful ways and live life separated from God—both now and forever.

The devil can't force people to do anything, but he uses his tactics of lies, deceits, and comparisons to try to get us to doubt ourselves or God. This has been going on since the Garden of Eden when the devil got Eve to question God by planting the seeds of doubt in her mind (Genesis 3:1, 4, 5). He didn't *force* her to go against God's instructions—but he convinced her to distrust them.

Similarly, the devil doesn't force you to push your sister or talk back to your parent or guardian. But he does try to plant those lies, those seeds of doubt, in your mind. Maybe your sister is annoying, so it's okay to push her . . . Or maybe your parent or guardian isn't being fair—after all, your friends get to do some things that you don't have permission to do.

But those are lies—and in direct contrast to what God tells you. Remember: "Do to others as you would have them do to you" (Luke 6:31). And also, "Above all, love each other deeply, because love covers over a multitude of sins" (1 Peter 4:8), meaning that you shouldn't push your sibling, even if they are annoying you. Likewise, God's Word tells you to "Honor your father and your mother" (Exodus 20:12), which means that you should respect them and their decisions.

The Bible gives many examples that demonstrate that the devil is our enemy and that he wants to destroy us. But do you know what the word "gospel" literally means? Gospel—the teachings of Jesus—translates to "good news." So, when we read the lessons of salvation through Christ in the Bible, we are reading the "good news." Trust the good (God), and tell the bad (the devil) to get away from you, and you will live a beautiful, full life. Amen!

1. James 4:7–8 gives us further direction on how we can push Satan away, and invite God to come near. "Submit yourselves, then, to God. Resist the devil, and he will flee from you. Come near to God, and he will come near to you." What are three things that you can do to resist the devil? What are three things you can do to come near to God?

2. One thing that was not discussed in this week's study was the importance of prayer. You will be tempted to sin. 1 Corinthians 10:13 tells us, "No temptation has overtaken you except what is common to mankind. And God is faithful; he will not let you be tempted beyond what you can bear. But when you are tempted, he will also provide a way out so that you can endure it." When you face temptation, call on God in prayer, and he will provide the way for you to "endure it" (overcome it). PRAY!

PRAYER

Dear God, it is scary to know that I have an enemy who is trying to separate me from you. But it's also good to be aware that my enemy is out there because it helps me to stay alert. Help me to stay connected to you through prayer and reading your Word so that I can resist the devil and stand firm in my faith. Thank you for giving me Jesus so that I can know with 100 percent certainty that even though there will be ups and downs in my life, through him, I've already won the overall war with the enemy. In Jesus's name. Amen.

WHY AM I HERE?

"Therefore go and make disciples of all nations, baptizing them in the name of the Father and of the Son and of the Holy Spirit, and teaching them to obey everything I have commanded you. And surely I am with you always, to the very end of the age."

MATTHEW 28:19-20

When you walk into your math class, you know exactly why you are there: to learn about math and practice applying what you learn by working through questions and equations that your teacher assigns. Likewise, when you go to church, you know that your purpose during that time is to learn about God and to worship alongside other people who share in your faith.

But what about overall in life? Why are any of us here, and what are we supposed to do with our lives?

This week, we read the final words recorded in the book of John, and they are Jesus's own words. He tells us to take his message to all nations, to baptize them, and to teach them to obey his commandments. After giving those instructions, he also reassures us that we won't be alone—ever. This reminds us that Jesus is with us even when we can't see him and that the Holy Spirit lives in us. What a comforting promise!

This reading from Matthew is known as the "Great Commission." When Jesus gives us this *commission*, it means he is giving us instructions—he is giving us our mission in life.

So how do we . . .

1. **Take Jesus's message to all nations**

2. **Baptize them**

3. **Teach them to obey his commandments**

Jesus answers this question in John 13:34–35: "A new command I give you: Love one another. As I have loved you, so you must love one another. By this, everyone will know that you are my disciples, if you love one another."

Love is the key. We start by living our lives with love.

If we do this, our kindness, caring, and compassion will open doors to connect with other people. That's what love does: it opens doors, opens people's hearts, and opens opportunities to share the good news of Jesus with others.

What that looks like will be a little bit different for each of us. Some people feel God's call to serve as pastors, some as teachers, some as accountants, some as husbands and fathers, some as farmers . . . As long as you do everything in love, it doesn't necessarily matter what you spend your time doing—you will be following Jesus's command (John 13:34–35), and opportunities will arise for you to fulfill Jesus's great commission (Matthew 28:19–20).

As a dearly loved child of God and follower of Jesus, you are here to live a godly life, which is quite simply a life of love. Start with that, and God will direct your paths in all things.

1. What are three things you can do each day to focus on living a life of love?

2. "All nations" can mean different countries around the world, but don't forget that even people in your own family or school are also included

in "all nations." How can you take Jesus's lessons (commands) every-where you go and share that information with those who you interact with? How can you do this at home? At school? With your friends?

3. Have you ever seen a baptism? What happens at a baptism? Why does Jesus tell us to baptize people in the name of the Father, Son, and Holy Spirit?

4. Jesus said, "And surely I am with you always, to the very end of the age." How does it make you feel to know that?

PRAYER

Dear Jesus, thank you for teaching me about your purpose for my life. Help me to always try to live a life of love so that I can spread your message everywhere I go. Thank you for assuring me that you will be with me always; that gives me so much comfort and peace. I lift this prayer up in your name. Amen.

PUTTING ON YOUR CLOTHES

**"Therefore, as God's chosen people, holy and
dearly loved, clothe yourselves with compassion,
kindness, humility, gentleness and patience."**

COLOSSIANS 3:12

How do you decide which clothes to wear each day? Do you have set
outfits for convenience? Is color coordination important to you? Do you
sometimes wear something special—like a shirt or jersey of your favorite
sports team or band? Is there a specific routine that you go about when
getting dressed each day?

No matter what you wear, it's important to choose the right clothes to
stay warm or cool, depending on the weather or environment. In a similar
way, our Bible verse this week tells us about some character qualities that
we should "clothe" ourselves with every day. These "clothes" are essential
for the *spiritual* environment that you will be in.

Here's something to try: As you are getting dressed each day, pause for
10 seconds and remind yourself to "put on" compassion, kindness, humility,
gentleness, and patience. You could even put a copy of this Bible verse on
a wall or mirror at home or in your locker at school so that every time you
read it, you'll remember to "wear" these qualities throughout your day.

Stop and think about the first part of this week's verse: "Therefore, as
God's chosen people, holy and dearly loved . . ." As a follower of Jesus, YOU
are one of God's chosen people, and YOU are holy and dearly loved. How
special is that?

When you are proud of the team you play on or the band that you
are in, you gladly wear your team jersey or band uniform to represent that

special group. Likewise, since you are part of God's chosen people, you should be super proud to represent God by "wearing" compassion, kindness, humility, gentleness, and patience. When you clothe yourself with these qualities, you show the world why God's team is the one that they should want to be on as well.

1. How does it make you feel to know that you are part of God's chosen people, and that you are holy and dearly loved?

2. Think about the qualities of compassion, kindness, humility, gentleness, and patience. What are some examples of ways that you can demonstrate (or "clothe" yourself in) these qualities each day?

3. How will you remind yourself to "put on" these qualities as part of your daily routine?

PRAYER

Dear Lord, thank you for counting me among your chosen people, holy and dearly loved by you. Please help me to bring honor and glory to you each day by clothing myself with qualities that would shine your light in the world. I ask this in Jesus's name, amen.

CALLING ON GOD

"Ask and it will be given to you; seek and you will find; knock and the door will be opened to you. For everyone who asks receives; the one who seeks finds; and to the one who knocks, the door will be opened."

MATTHEW 7:7–8

Legendary hockey player Wayne Gretzky said that you miss 100 percent of the shots you don't take, and that half the battle in achieving anything in life is simply showing up. Maybe you've heard the saying "Nothing ventured, nothing gained," which means that if you never take a risk, you will never reach your goals. The point of all these concepts is that those who dare to put themselves out there have a shot at accomplishing whatever it is they are attempting. On the other hand, those who shrink back and don't go for it (whatever "it" might be in a certain situation) may have an easier life, but they also miss out on receiving the reward they could have had if they'd just attempted "it."

Our verse this week brings a similar message. Jesus's words in Matthew 7 tell us that it will be given to us, we will find what we're looking for, and the door will be opened to us—but first, we have to ask, seek, and knock.

Here's a little trick to remember this: A.S.K. It represents the first letter of the three examples that Jesus uses when encouraging us to take action. Ask . . . Seek . . . Knock . . .

So if we miss 100 percent of the shots we don't take . . . let's shoot with confidence! If half the battle in life is simply showing up . . . let's show up every time, even when we don't feel like it. And if it's true that when nothing is ventured, nothing is gained . . . then let's take appropriate risks when there are potential rewards worth going for in life.

Jesus encourages us to live boldly, which is also the way that he lived, but he didn't expect us to do these things on our own. A.S.K.—it means that we are asking for help, leaning on God to assist us in our pursuits.

Encourage yourself to live with bold passion, but rest in the knowledge that you aren't expected to accomplish everything on your own. You have a loving heavenly Father who will respond whenever you ask. Always remember to A.S.K. for God's blessing in your life!

1. What does it mean to ask? What does it mean to seek? What does it mean to knock?

2. Jesus encourages us to live with bold passion. What does that tell us about God's nature?

3. How does it make you feel to know that Jesus essentially tells you that you will succeed when you lean on God as you ask, seek, and knock in life?

PRAYER

Heavenly Father, I know you don't want me to take risks just for the sake of living on the edge, but because there are times when beautiful blessings await those who have the strength to persevere through challenges. Please help me to live with bold passion and remind me that I can (and should) lean into you as I ask, seek, and knock. Thank you, God, for your encouragement and support. Amen!

SET an EHAMPLE

"Don't let anyone look down on you because you are young, but set an example for the believers in speech, in life, in love, in faith and in purity."

1 TIMOTHY 4:12

What examples do you follow in your life? Well, whether you realize it or not, you are influenced by dozens of factors on any given day. You see the examples of your parents or guardians, your coaches and teachers, and your pastor, to name only a few.

You're also influenced by TV, social media, books, friends, and stories you read in your Bible. We really are surrounded by examples in everything we do in life, but it's up to us to decide which ones we want to follow. As with most things, there are some "good" examples and some "bad" examples.

The focus of our verse this week isn't on the examples that you take in, but on the kind of example that you want to set for others.

But before we get into that, let's pause and look at the first part of the verse because it's really important. "Don't let anyone look down on you because you are young." Even though you can't control what others do or how they think, you shouldn't let it get to you if they try to dismiss you because of your youth. Bottom line: God values you very much, no matter your age. (See Matthew 19:14.)

Now, let's look at what type of example you should strive to set. Below are the areas of life that this week's verse tells us to set an example in, along with one Bible verse that relates to each area.

Speech: "Do not let any unwholesome talk come out of your mouths, but only what is helpful for building others up according to their needs, that it may benefit those who listen" (Ephesians 4:29).

Life: Read the Ten Commandments (Exodus 20).

Love: "Above all, love each other deeply, because love covers over a multitude of sins" (1 Peter 4:8).

Faith: "Trust in the Lord with all your heart and lean not on your own understanding; in all your ways submit to him, and he will make your paths straight" (Proverbs 3:5–6).

Purity: "Do you not know that your bodies are temples of the Holy Spirit, who is in you, whom you have received from God? You are not your own; you were bought at a price. Therefore honor God with your bodies" (1 Corinthians 6:19–20).

If you follow these concepts, you will indeed set a strong Christian example. But keep in mind that even when you do set a wonderful example, there will be those who think you are wrong or silly. They might even make fun of you. Don't be discouraged. Remember what Paul said in 1 Corinthians 11:1: "Follow my example, as I follow the example of Christ." Amen!

1. Have you ever experienced a situation where someone tried to dismiss you because you were young? How did that make you feel? How can you be prepared to persevere through that type of situation if it were to happen again?

2. Who are some people that you look to for solid Christian examples in your life?

3. Pick two of the areas of life from this week's verse (Speech, Life, Love, Faith, Purity), and think of ways that you can set an example in those areas this next week.

4. How did Jesus set an example in any of the areas mentioned in our verse this week?

PRAYER

Jesus, thank you for setting the ultimate example for me. Help me to look to you for how I should try to live. I want to be a good example so that I can point others to you. Thank you for all of your love and blessings. Amen.

THE WAY, THE TRUTH, THE LIFE

"Jesus answered, 'I am the way and the truth and the life.
No one comes to the Father except through me.'"

JOHN 14:6

Have you ever gone to an event where you had to pass through security to get into the venue? Think about a professional sporting event, a concert, some restaurants, hotels, the airport . . . All of these places have some sort of a checkpoint where the security person checks you and your baggage before permitting you to enter.

The Bible verse this week talks about another situation where there is only one way to enter a venue. And this verse isn't just talking about a concert or a fancy restaurant—it's talking about the most important place you could ever go and the most amazing presence you could ever come into. It's talking about being with God in his house, in heaven. Take a minute to soak that in.

Jesus tells us that there is only one way to come to the Father, and that is through him. Jesus is "the way" to get in!

If you go to a ballgame at a big stadium, at any given time there might be one hundred people coming into the stadium through one hundred different entrances. That is not the case with coming to our heavenly Father. There is one way, and that is through Jesus Christ. He is the truth if you are wanting to come into eternal life in heaven. Way, Truth, Life.

One more thing. Remember how we said that the security people check you and your baggage before you are permitted to enter a venue? In the spiritual world, "baggage" could mean some not-so-great things that we "carry around" with us in life—like a physical ailment, emotional pain, or stress. It also refers to our sins and the guilt that we carry because of them.

But Jesus isn't just the way into heaven. He also is the one who loves us so much that he takes away all of our heavy baggage and makes all things right.

1. What does Jesus mean when he says that he is "the way and the truth and the life"?

2. Why does no one come to the Father except through Jesus?

3. How does the verse this week help you understand why it is so important to accept Jesus Christ as your Lord and Savior? And why is it so important to spread this message throughout the world?

PRAYER

Dear God, I know that I make mistakes and am not good enough to come to your perfect heaven on my own. But I also know that you love me so much that you gave your Son, Jesus Christ, to be the way and the truth and the life, and that through him I can have eternal life with you in heaven. Please help me to always stay focused on that truth and to abide with Jesus every day. Amen.

OWNING UP TO MISTAKES

"If you hold to my teaching, you are really my disciples. Then you will know the truth, and the truth will set you free."

JOHN 8:31–32

Have you been in a situation where you tell a lie and the guilt of knowing that eats away at you? You feel bad about betraying someone's trust—or maybe the lie led to some bad outcome. You might be nervous that the lie will be found out, and you'll get in trouble. It's never easy to live with a lie.

The world that we live in is fallen, meaning that sin has become part of life on earth. The enemy of our souls wants to tempt us into believing that lies are OK—or that they're really the truth.

But only the truth is the truth. Jesus tells us in the verse this week that, "If you hold to my teaching, you are really my disciples. Then you will know the truth, and the truth will set you free."

And what does it mean to be set free? If you follow Jesus and his teachings, you will have the Holy Spirit helping you understand the difference between the devil's lies and God's truths. Knowing which is which sets you free to make the right choices—and making the right choices leads to living the best life.

Here's an example: Your parents ask whether you completed your homework, and you say yes, but you know that you really didn't do it all. Later, as you watch TV you feel really guilty for lying to them, especially when they say how proud they are of you for working so hard in school. That's a terrible feeling—knowing you have betrayed a loved one. You can either go on living that lie, or you can fess up and admit to what you did.

Yes, your parents will be disappointed, and there may be a consequence for lying. But in telling the truth, you will be doing the right thing, and your guilty conscience will be set free. You'll restore the relationship with your parents and learn a lesson not to lie anymore in the future.

Committing yourself to telling the truth will set you free, both now and forever.

1. What are some ways that you can hold to Jesus's teaching?

2. What does it mean to be a disciple of Jesus Christ, and how does that apply to your life?

3. What are examples of truth versus lies that you have experienced in your life?

4. What does it mean to you to be "set free" through God's truths?

PRAYER

Jesus, please help me to always know which way is the truth, and give me the strength to go in that direction even when a lie might seem like an easier choice. I want to be set free by living a truthful life on earth and join you for eternal life in heaven. I pray this in your name, amen.

EVERYTHING IS POSSIBLE

"With man this is impossible, but with God all things are possible."

MATTHEW 19:26

What would you do if you could do anything? I mean *anything* . . .

Would you join your favorite sports team, eat a pizza the size of a bicycle tire, fly to the moon and back, race a cheetah (and win), play video games for three days straight, play a concert in front of 30,000 people, or run across water? Maybe you would do something more service-focused, like heal sick people, give hungry children a lifetime supply of food, or help negotiate peace between world leaders.

It's pretty neat to think about all of the things you could do if there were no limits. But in this world, we have to learn to live within the boundaries of what is possible. That means, for instance, that you can't play for your favorite professional sports team as a kid. And humans can't fly like superheroes. Because we know these realities, we tend to limit our dreams and expectations to be more realistic. Instead of racing a cheetah, we just enjoy watching a cheetah blaze over the ground. Instead of trying to run across water, we jump in and go swimming.

Our Bible verse this week tells us that yes, for humans, some things are impossible. But "with God all things are possible." Just think about that for a moment . . . *all* things are possible.

That shouldn't be a surprise to us, right? God created everything that you see (including you)—not to mention lots of things you can't see. That's difficult to even imagine, but God has certainly given us a demonstration of why we should believe that he is capable of all things.

Take miracles, for instance. Have you ever read about or experienced one? A miracle is something that happens when science and logic tell us that thing is impossible. Yet miracles happen! The Bible is full of stories about God's miracles. Creating the world, parting the Red Sea, Daniel in the lion's den, Mary having Jesus, Jesus healing the sick, walking on water, and feeding thousands of people with only a few fish and loaves of bread . . . Jesus rising from the dead himself. We could go on and on. (Check out John 20:30–31.)

Thank God that even though he is capable of doing *all* things, he didn't just please himself by eating pizza or playing games. He used his creativity and love to create a whole universe, including you and me. So remember that no challenge you are facing is too big for God. You can always take your worries, concerns, and problems to him. He can do more than you could ever ask or imagine (Ephesians 3:20–21)!

1. How does it make you feel to know that all things are possible with God?

2. What are some of your favorite miracles from the Bible?

3. Have you experienced any miracles in your own life? How do you know if something is a miracle?

PRAYER

Dear God, thank you for reminding me that all things are possible for you, and that as your dearly loved child, I am blessed by miracles every day. Thank you! Amen.

FAITH SHARED IS FAITH MULTIPLIED

"Again, truly I tell you that if two of you on earth agree about anything they ask for, it will be done for them by my Father in heaven. For where two or three come together in my name, there am I with them."

MATTHEW 18:19-20

There is power in numbers. To change a law, legislators must get enough votes to pass their proposal. When a new sports team is formed, they base themselves in a city where the data shows they will be able to get a lot of fans to come to their games. The spotlight in life seems to follow the numbers—just look at the number of "likes" and "follows" on social media.

Our Bible verse this week is about that number power. Jesus encouraging his disciples to find common ground with each other and to pray together. These days, since Jesus doesn't physically live on earth with us, it's reassuring to know that God's presence and power will be with us whenever we join together to call on him.

It's been said that a faith shared is a faith multiplied. One of the challenges of the pandemic was that we couldn't always gather together in person. We like being with other people, and many of us struggled a bit with isolation and missed that sense of "community" we felt in one another's presence. Once we were able to come back together again, we rejoiced! (Read Hebrews 10:25.) When we get together to share worship and prayer—even if it has to be online—we grow in our faith.

So where might you join with others in Jesus's name? You can pray at home with your family, with friends in your neighborhood, or at church with your brothers and sisters in Christ. Youth groups can be great places to hang out with other kids your age and build community. There is power in numbers, and it is important to have Christian friends who can pray with you and help you make good choices. (Think about Ecclesiastes 4:12.)

Spend some time praying with others this week. You will experience the blessing of God's presence when you do.

1. How does it make you feel to know that when you call on Jesus's name, he will be there with you?

2. Group prayer is important, but God still hears (and cares about) your prayers even when it is just you praying by yourself. Jesus talks about a shepherd who has 100 sheep but loses one. That shepherd leaves the 99 other sheep to find the one that is lost and rejoices greatly when it is found. In the same way, God cares deeply about your individual prayers too. How can you balance spending time in group prayer with your own private prayer time?

3. When is one time this week you can plan to take part in a group prayer?

PRAYER

Heavenly Father, please help me to look for ways that I can connect with you in prayer, both with others and on my own. I'm so glad to know that Jesus is there with us when we pray! Thank you for all of your blessings. Amen.

SUPPORTING EACH OTHER

"As iron sharpens iron, so one person sharpens another."

PROVERBS 27:17

Do you know what a *blind spot* is? A blind spot is an area of weakness that you can't see about yourself, but that others see. We all have some blind spots in our own lives. Maybe we have a favorite shirt that we want to wear all the time, but we've worn it so much that it now has holes in it—holes we don't even notice. Or we might develop a habit of always picking the same class-mate first or last when assigning groups—not because we like or dislike that person more or less than the other students, but just because it has become a habit. Or think of a chess player who always does the same sequence of moves on the first four turns, making it easier for his opponent to win.

Maybe you're wondering why we're talking about blind spots when looking at this week's reading.

Those examples of blind spots I mentioned are all harmless, but they could be something that an outside person (maybe a friend or family member) would notice. Then they could gently point out our "holey" shirt, or team selection process, or chess moves to help us do better.

But there are also blind spots that are a little more serious, maybe even sinful. For example, maybe we get into the habit of using the Lord's name in ways that are not respectful and don't even realize we're doing it. (Even though the second commandment tells us not to do that.) Or maybe we like to get together with friends and share all the latest gossip, but we forget that gossiping is a sin that can hurt others.

Our verse this week is saying that we are to hold each other accountable for these blind spots—to help each other to live godly lives. That's how we "sharpen" one another. Maybe we have developed dangerous blind spots without even realizing it. But if a friend can see our blind spots and "speak the truth in love" (Ephesians 4:15), we can realize our errors and make corrections. Look for friends like that, and strive to be a friend like that to others. (Check out Hebrews 3:12–13.)

1. Who are three people you could help "sharpen" by being a supportive influence in their lives?

2. Who are three people who could help "sharpen" you in your life?

3. What are some potential spiritual "blind spots" that you have right now (aspects of your faith that might be weak but that you haven't thought of changing yet)?

PRAYER

Dear Lord, help me look for ways to stay connected to you and your Word so that I can remain sharp and also help sharpen others. Thank you for your love and blessings. In Jesus's name I pray, amen.

BY FAITH

"Now faith is confidence in what we hope for and assurance about what we do not see. This is what the ancients were commended for. By faith we understand that the universe was formed at God's command, so that what is seen was not made out of what was visible . . . These were all commended for their faith, yet none of them received what had been promised, since God had planned something better for us so that only together with us would they be made perfect."

HEBREWS 11:1–3, 39–40

Why do you do what you do? Almost always, we do things because they lead to a result that we desire. We wash our clothes because we want to wear clean clothes. We make a sandwich because we're hungry. We play a game because it's fun. But would you do things even if you didn't see an immediate reward for your effort?

Farmers do that all the time. After all, it takes months of work and patience to see the growing process through, from seed to harvest. Or consider someone who plants trees whose shade they will never enjoy— because it can take more than a lifetime for a tree to grow large enough to provide shade. Planting a tree to shade future generations is a selfless act because the planting doesn't directly benefit the planter.

That's what our Bible verses this week are about: living with faith, even when we don't see an immediate reward. Ancient people like Abel, Enoch, Noah, Abraham, Isaac, Jacob, Joseph, and Moses are recognized for their faith because they did what God asked of them even though they would never see the whole fulfillment of their efforts. (God had planned something better, for them and for us—and that something is Jesus—but that's a topic for another time.)

The point is, God desires for his people to have faith and to act accordingly, regardless of any reward or outcome that they'll receive in the moment. (Read 1 Corinthians 3:6–8.)

So why do you do what you do? Can you find a way to live by faith and to be a spiritual "farmer"? If you plant those seeds, God will take care of the rest. And don't worry about your reward; God's got something better planned for you on that front too!

1. What is something you are certain of but do not see (which is the definition of having faith)?

2. What is one thing that you can do to be a spiritual "farmer" and to support God's will by operating in faith?

3. What is the "something better" that God has planned for people who live by faith?

PRAYER

Dear heavenly Father, I hear your call to live by faith. Help me to know that doing your work, knowing that it pleases you, is more than enough reward for me. In Jesus's name I pray, amen.

WHAT'S YOUR REPUTATION?

"Even a child is known by his actions, by whether
his conduct is pure and right."

PROVERBS 20:11

Do you know what a reputation is? A reputation is basically a common perception that people have about somebody based on certain beliefs or opinions. For instance, is there a kid in your school who has a reputation for always getting in trouble? Or someone who is known for being really smart? Those are examples of reputations.

The Bible verse this week is a short thought from Proverbs, but it packs an important lesson. Even at your age, people are starting to form ideas about you based on your conduct—like the way you live and treat others and how trustworthy you are.

What type of reputation do you have? Are you known as someone who treats people with respect and kindness, someone who doesn't say swear words, and who demonstrates the fruit of the Spirit in their life? Or, have you made some mistakes and need more time to learn but unfortunately developed a reputation that you're not very proud of?

Step away from what other people think and, more importantly, what do you *want* your reputation to be? Our Bible verse this week provides the best answer. We all want our reputation to reflect a person whose conduct is pure and right. God has given you a conscience—the Holy Spirit—who teaches, corrects, and guides you so that you'll know the difference between right and wrong. Try your best to follow that guidance. When you do, you can be certain that you will build a good reputation.

Your reputation will also be formed, in part, by who you surround yourself with. If your friends have reputations as troublemakers, guess what people will think about you. Or if your friends are known as hard workers in class and in sports, guess what people will naturally assume about you.

Make sure Jesus is your best friend, and you will not only have a wonderful reputation, but you will live a beautiful life.

1. What kind of reputation do you have right now? Why?

2. What kind of reputation do you want to have? Why?

3. What things can you do to ensure that your reputation is what you want it to be?

4. What kinds of reputations do your friends have? What do you think about them?

5. What reputation does Jesus have? What do you think about it?

PRAYER

God, please help me to work every day to try to develop a reputation that points others to you in a positive way. I give thanks and praise to you in Jesus's name, amen.

MAKING GOD YOUR TOP PRIORITY

"Love the Lord your God with all your heart and with all your soul
and with all your strength. These commandments that I give you
today are to be on your hearts. Impress them on your children.
Talk about them when you sit at home and when you walk along
the road, when you lie down and when you get up. Tie them as
symbols on your hands and bind them on your foreheads. Write
them on the doorframes of your houses and on your gates."

DEUTERONOMY 6:5-9

What's the very first thing that you think about when you wake up in the morning? What's the last thing that you think about before you fall asleep at night? What is the topic that you talk about most often with your friends?

How you answer those questions will tell you a lot about what your priorities are. (Read Matthew 6:21.)

It's good to have a wide range of interests, and it's OK if you think about things other than God when you wake up, go to sleep, or talk with your friends. But there should be a healthy balance, and God should always hold an important place in your heart and mind. You'll grow more into this as you continue to mature in your faith. Eventually, a godly man will strive to love God with all of his heart, soul, and strength—which is a deep and powerful love.

But what about the rest of the thoughts shared in our verse this week? God gave Moses the Ten Commandments. Those commandments were so important that God wanted his people to keep them as their top priority—so much so that he told them to:

- Impress them on their children
- Talk about them when sitting at home, walking along the road, and when lying down and getting up
- Tie them as symbols on their hands and foreheads
- Write them on the doorframes and gates of their houses

God certainly made it clear how important it is for his people to prioritize his commandments! Remember, you are also one of God's people, and as you continue to grow, you'll need to create your own habits for living a godly lifestyle.

Start by trying to establish some routines around at least one of the thoughts included in our verses this week. Maybe you can make it a point to talk about God's Word for five minutes with your family at home each day, or read your Bible before going to sleep at night. Maybe you can set an alarm to remind yourself to pray in the morning, or draw a cross on your notebook as a reminder to keep God on your mind during your busy school day. Do you enjoy creating artwork? If so, you could design some sort of inspirational painting or sculpture that could be displayed somewhere at your home—maybe by the front door. These are just some practical ways that you could take steps to make God a bigger priority in your day and a more constant part of your thoughts.

1. What do you want your top five priorities (areas of focus) to be in life?

2. What are two things you can do this week to start to build routines that align with your priorities?

3. What does it mean to you to love God with all your heart, with all your soul, and with all your strength? What are some things you can do to make sure you are doing that every day?

PRAYER

Dear God, I want to continue to learn more about you and about how I can make you the top priority in my life. I'm going to look for ways that I can intentionally build things into my day that help me to stay focused on you. Please guide me in the choices I make. I ask this in Jesus's name, amen.

BaLancing PHYSicaL anD SPIRITUAL DeVeLOPMenT

"For physical training is of some value, but godliness has value for all things, holding promise for both the present life and the life to come."

1 TIMOTHY 4:8

If you work out consistently, you will build up strength and muscle mass. God blesses us with physical bodies, and it is important to take care of them to ensure that we are respecting that blessing.

Our Bible verse this week acknowledges that physical training is important, but it also highlights that godliness is even *more* important because godliness has value for *all* things, both in the present (earthly) life and in the life to come (in heaven). This is certainly a different opinion from what we see in mainstream culture, where physical training and sports are idolized and worshiped. (Look up 1 John 2:15–17.)

I don't care how strong your muscles are, if you don't regularly pick up your Bible, you will be weak.

Don't get me wrong: Sports are fun and a great way to spend time with friends while learning valuable life lessons such as training, teamwork, competition, perseverance, and how to handle winning and losing. But awards fade and trophies rust.

What never fades, rusts, or ends is a godly heart and lifestyle. God is more impressed by a good and humble person who tries their best and loses on the scoreboard than a person who does things that go against God's will but wins the game. The crowd might go wild over the person who scored the most points, but you aren't here to impress that crowd. As a Christian, you live your life to be celebrated by a crowd of one: God.

Enjoy sports and training if you are into those things. There are certainly plenty of benefits associated with the lessons that they offer, and God appreciates when people use their physical gifts in positive ways. But if you are faced with a decision between training and sports, and something that more closely aligns with God's will, choose the one that will benefit not only your present life but also have value for the life to come.

1. What is something you have done that would be considered physical training? Why did you do this activity?

2. What is something you have done that would be considered spiritual training? Why did you do this activity?

3. What is the "life to come," and how can you make sure that you are properly valuing it as you decide how to spend your time each day?

PRAYER

Heavenly Father, thank you for blessing me with interests and passions such as physical training and playing sports, but help me to always remember that it is even better to focus on godliness, as I know there is more value in living a life that brings honor and glory to you than winning a game on a scoreboard. In Jesus's name I pray, amen.

GOD'S GRACE

**"For it is by grace you have been saved, through faith—
and this not from yourselves, it is the gift of God—
not by works, so that no one can boast."**

EPHESIANS 2:8–9

The biblical concept of "grace" is defined as the undeserved favor of God toward humans. Can you think of any examples when your parents or guardians may have given you grace? Maybe there was a time when you were told that if you wanted to go to your friend's house later, you would need to do a chore first, such as cleaning your room. You agreed to do it but then got distracted, and when the time came to go to your friend's house, you still hadn't gotten around to the chore. Your parents or guardians *could* have said that you were no longer allowed to go, since you hadn't completed your side of the bargain. But instead, knowing that your friend had that new video game that the two of you had been looking forward to playing together, they gave you permission to go anyway. That's an example of grace—undeserved favor.

God's grace is similar. He gives us his favor even when we don't deserve it, and it flows from his great love for us. (Read Romans 5:8.) Our Bible verse this week says that it is by this grace—this "gift of God"—that we have been saved. But God doesn't force the gift on us. He gives us free will to choose whether we will accept it—and accept the ultimate gift of grace, Jesus our Savior.

Our Father in heaven loves to give us gifts. The ultimate gift is the route to salvation through Jesus Christ. Because we could never deserve or earn that kind of gift, we can't boast about how great we are to win such a treasure. Instead, we boast about how great *God* is to give it. Amen!

(Want to know more? Check out 2 Corinthians 12:9 and 2 Corinthians 10:17.)

1. What is an example of when you have experienced grace *from* another person?

2. What is an example of when you have given grace *to* another person?

3. What does it mean in 2 Corinthians 12:9 when it says, "My grace is sufficient for you"?

4. How can you "boast in the Lord" (2 Corinthians 10:17)?

PRAYER

Dear God, thank you for the loving grace that you extend to me in so many ways, and most clearly through the gift of your Son, and my Savior, Jesus Christ. Help me to find ways that I can share your grace with others. In Jesus's name I pray, amen.

CHOOSE WISELY

"...then choose for yourselves this day whom you will serve...
But as for me and my household, we will serve the Lord."

JOSHUA 24:15

As you continue to get older, you will start to experience more and more freedoms, as well as the responsibilities that come with them. Some examples are driving a car, choosing what you want to eat during the day, setting your own bedtime, and deciding what you want your next step to be after high school graduation. Some of these freedoms are more immediate decisions (what will you eat for lunch), while others stretch out over a longer period of time (what will you do with your life once you complete school).

Sir Isaac Newton's third law of motion tells us that "for every action there is an equal and opposite reaction." Similarly, while you may have greater freedoms as you continue to grow up, there will also be bigger and bigger consequences for the decisions that you make. Those consequences could be things such as cavities if you eat too many sugary foods, or not being able to get into the college of your choice if you don't work hard enough in school to get good grades. Some decisions have more lasting consequences than others, but every decision in life has some level of impact on how your life moves forward.

Joshua exhibited strong godly leadership and put his faith in the one true God. This decision led his family, both at that time and in their future generations, to be God's people and receive the blessings that went along with that. Some of the Israelites decided to follow other false gods. They put their trust and faith in created things that had no true power, and so in turn, their lives, both at that time and through future generations, suffered accordingly.

As a young man of God, and as you continue to grow into a man of God, what are you going to rely on to help you make decisions in life? Are you going to go with the crowd? (There are challenges in that—see Matthew 7:13–14.) Or are you going to make decisions based on what you learn in God's Word and through prayerful consideration? (Read Proverbs 3:5–6.)

Choose wisely. Choose God.

1. What does it mean to serve the Lord through your decisions? Can you think of any examples of ways that you have done this in your life?

2. Have you seen your parents/guardians making decisions? What do they rely on to help them?

3. What are three decisions that you will face this week? How will you decide what to do?

4. What are three decisions that you will face in the next 10 years? How will you decide what to do?

PRAYER

Dear Lord, as I continue to grow up, I know that there will be small decisions that I need to make about everyday life, as well as big decisions about my future. Give me strength and guidance to navigate these choices. I love you, and I have full faith that when I let go and trust you, you will make my paths straight. Thank you. In Jesus's name, amen.

CO-CREATING YOUR LIFE WITH GOD

**"In their hearts humans plan their course, but
the Lord establishes their steps."**

PROVERBS 16:9

Calling your shot has become a more common thing in sports, and life, over the last few decades. Babe Ruth had one of the most famous "called shots" in history. Legend has it that in the fifth inning of Game 3 in the 1932 World Series, Ruth pointed toward the flagpole in center field. On the next pitch, the Babe hit a towering home run near the flagpole, an estimated 490 feet from home plate.

What shots are you calling in your life? Are you planning to go to college, get married, work in a specific job, or live in a certain city?

Think about and plan for the future. Have dreams. But our Bible verse this week reminds us that, as godly people, it's also important to seek the Lord's will in our lives. In your heart you can plan your course, but there will come a time when you should bend a knee to the Lord and allow him to determine your steps.

Remember this verse: "Now listen, you who say, 'Today or tomorrow we will go to this or that city, spend a year there, carry on business and make money.' Why, you do not even know what will happen tomorrow . . . Instead, you ought to say, 'If it is the Lord's will, we will live and do this or that'" (James 4:13–14, 15).

If it is the Lord's will.

This brings us to the concept of "co-creating" your life with God. You see, we are not meant to just sit in a chair all day waiting for God to give us something to do in life. But we also shouldn't go out and say that we are going to do this, this, this, and this—without seeking God's will and making sure that whatever we plan is in alignment with his call to us. There should be a healthy balance of co-creation between us and the Lord. And, spoiler alert, his ways are better and higher than ours, so if you are feeling conflicted at all, bend a knee to God. You will always be glad that you did, and things will turn out for the best.

"Commit to the Lord whatever you do, and he will establish your plans" (Proverbs 16:3).

1. Have you called any shots with regard to what your plans are for your life in the future? If so, what plans have you developed?

2. What are some ways that you can be sure you are seeking God's will in your life?

3. What are some areas of life that you think you may want to start building plans for the future? How can you be sure to include God in this process?

PRAYER

Heavenly Father, Son, and Holy Spirit, thank you for giving me interests, skills, hopes, and dreams that make me who I am and give me fun things to look forward to in life. I know that it isn't right for me to only pursue the things that make me happy—I also want to seek your will and use my abilities to serve you. I want to co-create my life with you. Make of me what pleases you. Amen.

HeaRTS anD MINDS

"Since, then, you have been raised with Christ, set your hearts on things above, where Christ is seated at the right hand of God. Set your minds on things above, not on earthly things."

COLOSSIANS 3:1-2

Have you ever been so excited about something that you couldn't sleep? Maybe Christmas or a visit from a loved one you haven't seen in a while? Or maybe a big game or concert, or a special family trip? Whatever it was, if you know what it's like to be so excited about something that you can't even think about anything else, then you can understand the focus of our Bible verses this week.

Let's take a closer look. "Since, then, you have been raised with Christ,"—that's a reminder of the victory that is ours thanks to Jesus. Because of his perfect life, innocent death, and triumphant resurrection, we get to "raise" with him, and spend our eternal life in heaven with him, our absolute best friend. "Set your hearts on things above" means that we should set our hope and faith—our excitement—on the promises of heaven, "where Christ is seated at the right hand of God."

We are reminded that we have been "raised with Christ" and encouraged to set our hearts on heaven. Our reading goes on to say, "Set your minds on things above, not on earthly things." That means we are to set both our hearts *and* our minds on "things above." That's a pretty clear message, huh? We should focus our hearts and minds on heavenly things over earthly things.

Let's go back to the beginning of our discussion this week—about things that make us so excited that we can't sleep or focus on anything else. Getting to live our eternal life in our forever home of heaven with our best friend Jesus is that kind of thing if you really think about it. (Check out what Paul says in Philippians 3:17–21.) Just imagine how awesome that will be!

So set your hearts and minds on heaven. What could be more exciting?

"Let everything that has breath praise the Lord. Praise the Lord" (Psalm 150:6).

1. What is an example of a time when you were so excited that you couldn't sleep or focus on anything else?

2. We are told over and over again in the Bible that heaven is a place of perfection, it is God's home and through Jesus it will be ours as well. We will get to live forever in paradise and in direct fellowship with God. Amazing! God's people on earth really should spend more time looking forward to heaven. What are some things that you can do to help get yourself excited about heaven?

3. What does it mean to you to set your heart and mind on something? How can you apply that same feeling toward your faith?

PRAYER

Almighty God, help me to set my heart and mind on the things of heaven. Show me how I can grow in my relationship with you and build up my excitement for living with you in heaven. I pray this in Jesus's name, amen.

OUR SUPPORT SYSTEM

"Therefore, since we are surrounded by such a great cloud of witnesses, let us throw off everything that hinders and the sin that so easily entangles. And let us run with perseverance the race marked out for us, fixing our eyes on Jesus, the pioneer and perfecter of faith."

HEBREWS 12:1–2

Think of the biggest crowd of people that you've ever performed in front of. Maybe it was for a championship soccer game or a school play, or maybe you were picked out of the audience to come up front and take part in a group challenge. At some point, everyone gets up in front of some sort of audience. I bet yours was probably cheering you on.

During the pandemic, one of the craziest things professional athletes experienced was competing in empty stadiums, since crowds couldn't gather together. Imagine: these top athletes who were used to being energized by the cheers of thousands of fans were suddenly playing in silent venues. It took some getting used to, but the athletes knew their fans were still cheering them on from a distance.

Think about the people who are cheering *you* on from a distance. Maybe a grandparent or other loved one sent you a message before your big event, telling you that they couldn't be there in person but that they would be cheering from afar. Even if they weren't physically with you, could you still somehow *feel* their support? Did it bring you comfort and inspiration knowing that they were praying for you to do well? (Read 1 Corinthians 5:3.)

Our verse this week talks about supporters that you might not even know you have, who have been cheering you on throughout your entire life. The Bible calls these supporters a "great cloud of witnesses." A *witness* is someone who is present to see something happen. In our case, the witnesses are people who have seen and experienced God's love through Jesus, and who surround us to teach us about God's love and cheer us on to godly living and the ultimate victory of entering heaven to be with Jesus, the "pioneer and perfecter of our faith."

Next time you're feeling alone, remember that there is a whole crowd of supporters around you, cheering you on!

1. What's a time when you have felt surrounded by a crowd of supporters (sporting event, performance, etc.)? How did that make you feel?

2. How does it feel to know that you have a spiritual crowd of supporters cheering you on? How could this unseen support impact your life moving forward?

3. What are some ways that you can be sure you are supporting your friends and loved ones?

PRAYER

Dear Lord, the more I learn about you and grow in my faith, the more I see how much you love me and how you are there to support me in so many ways. Thank you for encouraging me through a great cloud of witnesses. Amen.

THE GOLDEN RULE: FORGIVENESS

"Be kind and compassionate to one another, forgiving each other, just as in Christ God forgave you."

EPHESIANS 4:32

Do you know the "Golden Rule"? Jesus shared it in Matthew 7:12 when he said, "So in everything, do to others what you would have them do to you." Basically, it means treating others the way you would want to be treated. And this same idea applies to forgiving others when they make a mistake.

Can you think of a time you made a mistake? Maybe you said or did something selfish or rude—or maybe there was something that you *didn't* say or do, such as helping a friend when they were getting teased. Whatever the case, we all know what it's like to feel sorry—when the thing that we want most is to be forgiven. If the person we wronged does forgive us, we are grateful and make sure that we don't make that same mistake again. Being forgiven is a wonderful, freeing feeling.

But what about when someone wrongs you? Are you quick to give that person the same level of forgiveness that you value so much when you're on the receiving end? Even though we know how powerful it is to *receive* forgiveness, it can be difficult to *extend* forgiveness to someone who has hurt us. But that's exactly what our Bible verse this week is challenging us to do.

"Be kind and compassionate to one another, forgiving each other." That makes sense, right? But it's the final part of our verse that really sets the Christian lifestyle apart: "just as in Christ God forgave you." There it is. The forgiveness that we receive from God for our own sins comes through

Jesus's loving sacrifice—and it's pretty difficult to hold a grudge against someone else when we remember that Jesus died on the cross for our sins.

And this brings us full circle, getting us back to the Golden Rule. "So in everything, do to others what you would have them do to you." If you appreciate the wonderful, freeing feeling that comes from being forgiven, then you must try to extend that same level of forgiveness to others when they wrong you. When that's hard to do, remember our ultimate example of forgiveness—when God forgave us of our sins through Jesus Christ, our Lord and Savior. (Check out 1 Peter 4:8.)

Demonstrate God's love to others; forgive as you have been forgiven.

1. What is one thing that you could do to make sure you are treating others the way you would like to be treated? (For example, at recess, during lunch, after school, at practice.)

2. Why does it feel so good to be forgiven when you make a mistake? How can you let someone know that they hurt your feelings, but that you still forgive them?

3. How can you remind yourself of the blessing of forgiveness that you receive each day through Jesus Christ? What does God's forgiveness mean to you eternally?

PRAYER

Gracious God, thank you for loving me, and forgiving me, through Jesus. Help me to extend forgiveness to others, in Jesus's name. Amen.

HUNTING, FISHING, AND FOOD

**"Man shall not live on bread alone, but on every
word that comes from the mouth of God."**

MATTHEW 4:4

We all need food, right? Yes, that is a physical truth of our earthly bodies.
But as is so often the case with the ways of God, we must understand that
there is also a *spiritual* side to our existence. Big topic for sure, but let's look
at what the Bible has to say about hunting, fishing, and food.

Hunting: "The lazy man does not roast his game, but the diligent man
prizes his possessions" (Proverbs 12:27). "The lazy man does not roast
his game . . ." Maybe this guy is so lazy that he won't even go hunting,
so he has no food. Or maybe he's just too lazy to cook it, which would
mean eating raw meat (which could make him sick). Either way, being
lazy is not a good way to feed yourself. On the other hand, a "diligent
man"—a hard worker—values and appreciates the things he is blessed
with, including his food.

Fishing: "Come, follow me," Jesus said, "and I will make you fishers of
men" (Matthew 4:19). Several of Jesus's first disciples were fishermen. It
was how they earned their living. Jesus used the example of fishing to
help them understand what it would be like to be his disciples and to
work to bring other people into the ministry. Have you done any fishing
in your life? From a ministry perspective, have you ever been a "fisher"
of others, as you tried to "catch" them to be followers of Jesus Christ?

Food: "Man shall not live on bread alone, but on every word that comes from the mouth of God." No matter what kinds of food we eat, we also need to "feed" our spiritual health. If you want to "hunt" or "fish" for spiritual food, read your Bible and spend time thinking and praying about what God is telling you.

Most of us have experienced physical hunger, to the point where our stomachs growl. But what does it mean to be hungry from the spiritual side? When your spirit "growls," try opening your Bible to "feed" your soul. Start establishing a routine for reading your Bible and start choosing some of your favorite verses!

Go ahead and hunt and fish. Do it to fill your stomach. But also remember the lessons that the Bible teaches about "hunting" and "fishing" to feed your soul. (Read 2 Timothy 3:16–17.)

1. What are some of your favorite foods (that fuel your body)?

2. What are some of your favorite Bible verses (that fuel your soul)?

3. What lessons do you take from Proverbs 12:27?

4. What lessons do you take from Matthew 4:19?

5. How can you balance your physical and spiritual feedings each day?

PRAYER

Heavenly Father, you give me everything that I need to live. Help me to make time to feed not only my body, but my soul as well. In Jesus's name I pray, amen.

YOUR MOMENT WITHIN GOD'S TIMING

**"And who knows but that you have come to your
royal position for such a time as this?"**

ESTHER 4:14

Picture it: Your team is losing by three runs, the bases are loaded, it's the bottom of the last inning, there are two outs . . . and YOU are the batter. This next pitch could be the final pitch of the game—if you get out, your team loses. But if you hit a home run, your team will win.

Even if you aren't a baseball player, you probably understand this kind of high stakes, win-or-lose situation. Everything is on the line, and what happens next comes down to you. Have you ever experienced something like that?

Our verse this week talks about one of those big moments in life. The book of Esther tells the story of Esther becoming queen, even though she was an unlikely choice (she was a Jewish person in a part of the world where Jews were a minority). Esther was a beautiful young woman, but no one—not even Esther herself—would expect her to become a leader who would save her people. However, Esther was exactly who God used to do just that. God had confidence in Esther even if she didn't feel ready to face the big moment she found herself in.

This would be like your coach putting you into that baseball game at the very biggest moment and letting you know he had 100 percent confidence that YOU could hit that home run. Maybe you didn't see the winning qualities in yourself, but your coach knew you could do it.

It was much the same for Esther. She found herself queen of a large empire where Jewish people—her people—faced persecution. But she had come to this royal position "for such a time as this." She prayed for courage and followed through and actually managed to save the Jewish people.

Have you had any such moments in your life where you faced an unexpected challenge and wondered if you were up to it? Now is a great time to start preparing your heart and mind to be ready for *big moments* like that. Remember, you don't have to face them alone. Call on God, and trust that he has you there "for such a time as this."

1. Have you ever experienced a moment that you can look back on now and see that God had brought you there for "such a time as this"?

2. Have you ever experienced a similar moment on a smaller scale, such as at a sporting event?

3. Check out Luke 12:11–12 and Exodus 14:13–14. How do the messages from these verses make you feel? What message does God give to us through verses such as these?

PRAYER

Heavenly Father, it is humbling to think that you would consider using me to lead and serve others at big moments in life. I know that when you call on me, you will be with me and help me know what to say and do. Thank you for your love and guidance always, amen.

A LIFE OF JOY, PEACE, AND HOPE

"May the God of hope fill you with all joy and peace as you trust in him, so that you may overflow with hope by the power of the Holy Spirit."

ROMANS 15:13

What are some words you would use to describe a man? Maybe strong, tall . . . has facial hair, drives a car, has a job . . . Yes, those can be accurate. But remember, while *we* might look at outward things to describe a man, *God* looks at the inner qualities.

"The Lord does not look at the things people look at. People look at the outward appearance, but the Lord looks at the heart" (1 Samuel 16:7).

Some very wonderful inner qualities and blessings are wished for us in our verse this week—that we would be filled with joy and peace, and overflow with hope through the power of the Holy Spirit. And if we are to live by the power of the Holy Spirit, then our lives will bloom with the fruit of the Spirit.

Remember, "the fruit of the Spirit is love, joy, peace, patience, kindness, goodness, faithfulness, gentleness and self-control" (Galatians 5:22–23).

So there we have it, a list of inward qualities that godly men will exhibit:

- From Romans 15:13—Joy, Peace, Trust, Hope
- From Galatians 5:22–23—Love, Joy, Peace, Patience, Kindness, Goodness, Faithfulness, Gentleness, Self-Control

It boils down to a life of joy, peace, and hope. (I would also add faith and love to our list—see 1 Corinthians 13:13 for more insight.)

Write down a list of both outward and inward qualities that you would like to develop as you grow. Put that list where you will see it frequently—maybe in your room or locker. Ask God to help you work on developing those qualities. Eventually, add Bible verses to your list, and catch a vision of the godly man you want to become. Start there, and pray for God to help you expand upon your list over the years. Who knows? You might even start clapping your hands and turn your list into a song!

"Clap your hands, all you nations; shout to God with cries of joy" (Psalm 47:1).

1. What are three outward qualities that you would like to develop as you grow into becoming a man?

2. What are three inward qualities that you would like to develop as you grow into becoming a man?

3. What would a life of joy, peace, and hope look like for you as a 14-year-old? As an 18-year-old? As a 25-year-old?

PRAYER

Dear God, it's exciting to think about my future. Please help me to think about what kind of inner qualities I would like to develop as I grow. Thank you for giving me examples of these qualities through the Bible, and for the security of knowing that my identity is rooted in Jesus. Amen.

In a Pickle (or Belly)

"Those who cling to worthless idols turn away from God's love for them. But I, with shouts of grateful praise, will sacrifice to you. What I have vowed I will make good. I will say, 'Salvation comes from the Lord.'"

JONAH 2:8-9

Have you ever avoided doing something that you knew your parents or guardians wanted you to do? Maybe it was delivering a message to your teacher, or including the new kid at school in your group at lunch. Or possibly they told you to choose the healthier option in the cafeteria, but when the time came, you found it hard to grab the vegetables instead of the dessert. If you keep disobeying your parents or guardians—and they find out about it—you are likely to face some negative consequences (also known as being in trouble). Sometimes, people use the phrase "in a pickle," to describe a situation like that.

Our Scripture verse this week is taken from the book of Jonah, which tells the story of a person who is in one of the biggest pickles of all time. Jonah ends up in the belly of a giant fish—and he stays in there for three days and nights!

Here's what happened: God asked Jonah to go to the city of Nineveh to tell the people to repent their sins. But Jonah did *not* want to go—so he didn't. So God sent the great fish to swallow Jonah—putting him into a *serious* time-out. In the fish's belly, Jonah had plenty of time to be still and think about the decisions he'd been making. He realized his mistake and gave in to God's call upon his ministry. Our Bible verse this week records the last few sentences of Jonah's apology prayer.

Jonah realized that anything other than serving God is "worthless" and that those who do that give up "God's love for them." Look at the rest of Jonah's prayer: "But I, with a song of thanksgiving, will sacrifice to you. What I have vowed I will make good. Salvation comes from the Lord."

That means that when you skip dessert and eat those vegetables, you can do so with shouts of grateful praise and a heart that says, "I trust that the vegetables will be better for my health, and that my parents/guardians have a plan that is good for my life."

But you can't just *tell* your parents/guardians that you'll choose the vegetables. You have to follow through when you get into that cafeteria line. "What I have vowed I will make good" means you keep your promises.

The final part of Jonah's prayer, "Salvation comes from the Lord," reminds us that no matter what direction God calls us to in life, our salvation comes from him through Jesus.

Want to know what happened right after Jonah finished his prayer to God? "And the Lord commanded the fish, and it vomited Jonah onto dry land." After that, you can bet Jonah followed God's instructions, went to Nineveh, and preached to the people.

Next time you find yourself in a pickle, pray for direction and follow God's call. It's the right way to live, and it is far better than being in the belly of a fish! (Or in a time-out.)

1. What is one situation where you have found yourself in a pickle? Were you in trouble with your parents/guardians or in trouble at school? What did you do to get into trouble? How was the issue resolved?

2. What main lesson do you take from the story of Jonah?

3. What apology prayer would you say if you were in a really difficult situation and you knew you needed God's forgiveness?

4. How can you use the lesson from the Bible study this week to help you avoid getting into trouble in the future?

PRAYER

Heavenly Father, I know that your ways are right and true, and that I should follow you at all times. Help me to be better at doing this, and to be quick to offer up a prayerful apology when I get into a pickle. In Jesus's name, amen.

ACKNOWLEDGMENTS

Praise be to God the Father, Son, and Holy Spirit, for the good news of salvation through Jesus Christ and for your living Word (the Bible). All honor and glory to you, Lord!

To my wife, Sarah, for all of your love and support as I worked through this project. I would not be able to accomplish anything of meaning without God's blessings and your love. You are my hero!

To all of the boys who I have had the privilege of coaching in sports and other groups/clubs. Thank you for the opportunity to serve you through those programs, and for inspiring me as I wrote this book. Remember to seek and follow the Lord in everything that you do, and you will thrive in your lives as men of God.

> *"For this reason, since the day we heard about you, we have not stopped praying for you. We continually ask God to fill you with the knowledge of his will through all the wisdom and understanding that the Spirit gives, so that you may live a life worthy of the Lord and please him in every way: bearing fruit in every good work, growing in the knowledge of God, being strengthened with all power according to his glorious might so that you may have great endurance and patience, and giving joyful thanks to the Father, who has qualified you to share in the inheritance of his holy people in the kingdom of light."* (Colossians 1:9–12)

God's blessings to you always!

–SH

ABOUT THE AUTHOR

SHANE HANSEN is a disciple of Jesus Christ, a husband, a father, and an entrepreneur. He is an International Coach Federation (ICF)–trained life coach and graduate of the Certified Professional Life Coach (CPLC) program through the Christian Coach Institute. He also holds a bachelor's and master's degree in business administration. Shane helps his brothers and sisters in Christ co-create their journey with the Lord, so that they can live intentional and impactful lives aligned with God's purpose and abiding in His peace. He has served as a Christian life coach, author, and speaker since 2015. Parents, for more about Shane, visit shanehansenclc.com.

Hi, parents and caregivers,

We hope your child enjoyed *Preteen Devotional for Boys*. If you have any
questions or concerns about your book, or have received a damaged
copy, please contact customerservice@penguinrandomhouse.com.
We're here and happy to help.

Also, please consider writing a review on your favorite retailer's website
to let others know what your preteen thought of the book!

Sincerely,
The Zeitgeist Team